The Gate of Choice

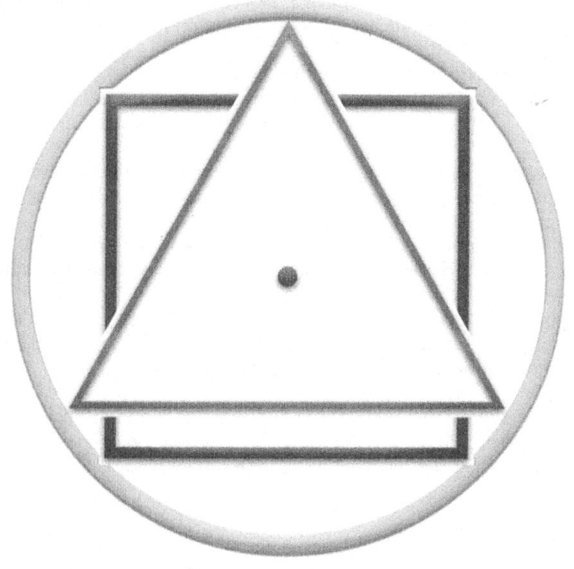

A Dictionary for the Higher Human

By Pejman Ghadimi

The Gate of Choice
A Dictionary for the Higher Human
Secret Consulting, INC
www.GateofChoice.com

Published by Secret Consulting INC, Delray Beach, Florida.

Secret Consulting, INC publishes in a variety of electronic formats. Some content in print may be available in electronic books. For more info on electronic versions of this book as well as other books and eBooks available by Secret Consulting, INC, visit www.GateofChoice.com

1st Edition
ISBN: 978-1-7346827-1-7

Hardbound Edition
ISBN: 978-1-7346827-2-4

Printed in United States of America.

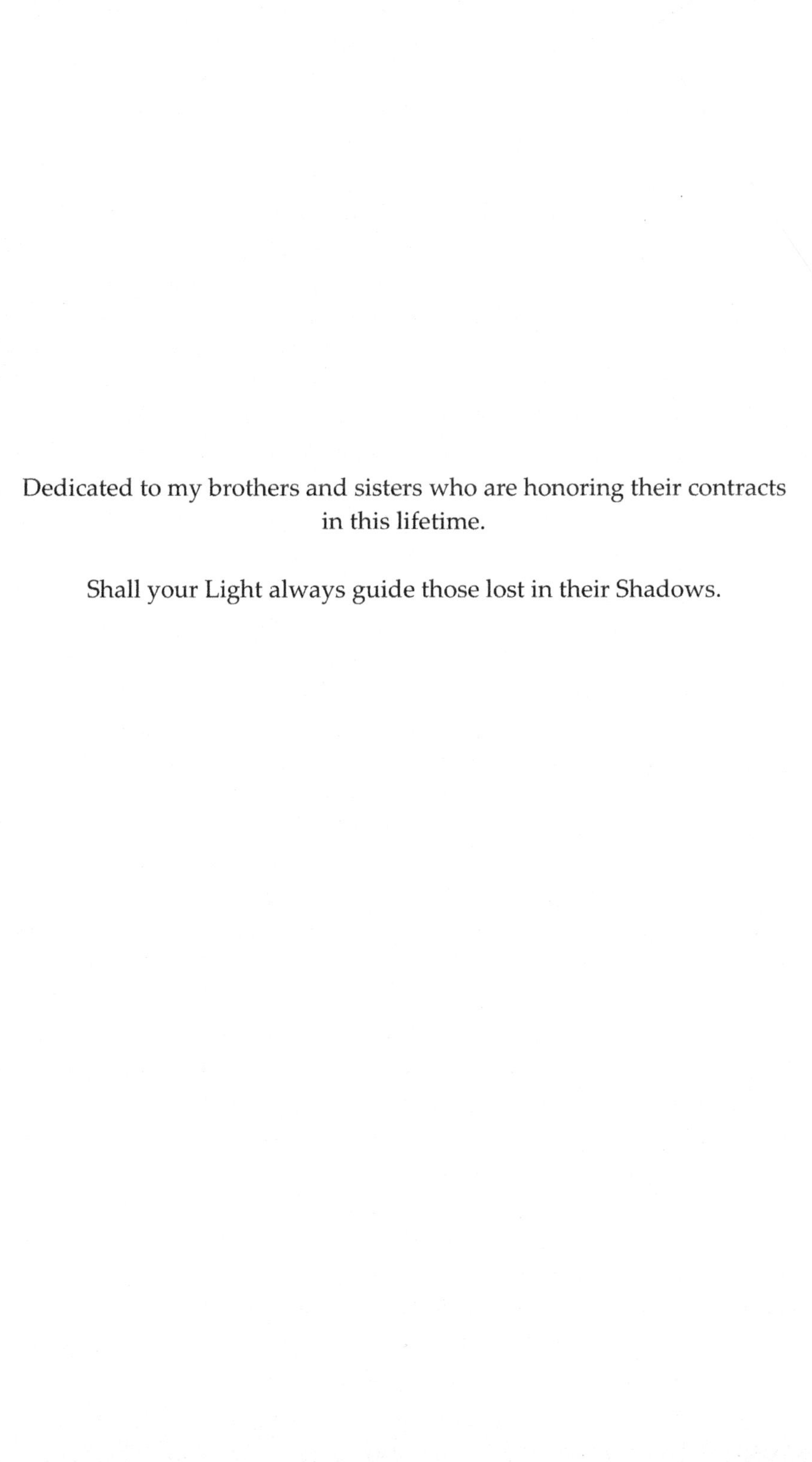

Dedicated to my brothers and sisters who are honoring their contracts in this lifetime.

Shall your Light always guide those lost in their Shadows.

Table of Contents

Preface

The world is changing, and it is changing quickly. From business to politics to spirituality. The rules of how people think—and what we think of—are changing. Our understanding of each other, our beliefs, our function are changing and, as a result, the rules of existing are also becoming blurred with the rules of living.

As humans, we wonder, what is the purpose of our existence?

Is there something greater?

Is there a bigger reason we exist?

Is it God?

Is it the universe?

Is it energy that guides us?

How can we even explain the invisible forces and events that occur in our lives in such perfectly synchronized manners?

How can random horoscopes based on stars, dates, or time be so accurate? How can karmic paths be so descriptive? And how can others foresee our future when it has yet to occur? We often wonder if there is such a thing as free will. How can so many aspects of who we are or what happens to us already be written?

We question our free will, our existence, and what happens past our existence. We even question if we have been here before in another life and why certain things seem more familiar than others.

This never-ending rabbit hole brings up two important questions:

Are we indeed the product of engineers, or was it simply evolution?

If we have been engineered, then how do we evolve and why?

In our attempt to discover our "WHY," or the purpose of our existence, we create what we call a parameter of living life. In other words, we create an internal matrix or a "bubble" as some refer to it. We create a world of truth based on our understanding of definitions we have been raised with, taught over time, and have learned to accept and live by. We believe these definitions to be our absolute truth (our boundary of control). A convincing truth we have allowed to define our existence and give it meaning.

The idea of pre-established definitions is a curious one. We spend our entire lives searching for various ways to define our own lives—for individuality, for impact and for greater consciousness. Yet, all of our searches rely on a set of definitions that were established hundreds of years ago by individuals who shared a minuscule percentage of our capacity as humans. They had yet to experience the vast amount of collective information that is available today.

So, why do we continue to rely on these so-called "definitions" rooted so far back in history, rather than establish new ones?

Partly because we, as humans, can only exist when structure exists in our lives. Often we can't make sense of the idea that without a beginning, or an end, we cannot seem to understand where we fit in. Boundaries and structure provide useful parameters, enabling us to understand where we begin and where we end, from both a physical standpoint and a spiritual one. Definitions, per se, are the boundaries we use to give meaning to words. However, we have never really stopped to think that perhaps these same boundaries are restrictive. Are they the reason we don't advance in life?

Our inability to rewrite and redefine our understanding is the limitation we have created for ourselves and never questioned.

This thought leads us to the core idea behind *The Gate of Choice*.

This book is based on new definitions, a new understanding of life here on earth, and of theological evolution. A book whose meaning for you will change as you evolve. It will guide you when you need a shift in perspective. This is a dictionary for those of a higher vibration who seek to gain a new perspective of their cosmic purpose. *The Gate of Choice* is also a dictionary for those who have yet to be in touch with their spiritual self, in hopes that the structure the book creates around this topic will fortify an opportunity to gain more wisdom.

Man has always been a prisoner of his mind and his thoughts. While some men have been able to break free of their own shadow and then able to live rather than exist, all men on earth are prisoners of time. Time is the ultimate boundary of control that no man has ever been able to break free of.

By the end of this book, you will understand why time is not a boundary of control, but rather the ultimate lesson that man must master as he undertakes various roles, karmic paths, and personalities. You will understand that time isn't just relative; it is, rather, its own dimension—one that is experienced very differently based on where you exist in space, and, even more importantly, HOW you exist.

Do not forget that *The Gate of Choice* will have a different meaning for all men; I say "man" as non-binary human beings and all variations of being a human, holding no regard for gender, race, disability, or any other societal construct that has made us believe that we are not all but one. I only use this singularity in the book in hopes of keeping its messaging free from validation, and instead give you an opportunity to identify with its message as a human free of judgment.

At various stages of your evolution, *The Gate of Choice* will continue to open your mind to new definitions, perspectives, and truths. When combined in the correct order with my previous books, *Third Circle Theory* and *RADIUS*, I believe *The Gate of Choice* becomes the most complete dictionary for modern man to use for dealing with the complicated aspect of being human. More importantly, this knowledge forms a precise roadmap to enabling each and every one of us an opportunity to progress to a new state of dimensional awareness. This opportunity may scare those in control of our society, as adopting such a way of life would mean to overcome the control mechanisms that have been placed to force us to accept comfort over evolution.

While this book may seem complicated and will require you to reread certain sections, please remember that at each stage of your evolution, it will hold a very different meaning.

I recommend that you first read *Third Circle Theory* and *RADIUS* in order to keep intact that this content is a progression; you can't just jump to the end. My purpose in writing this book is not to make you change the way you live or prescribe you a new control mechanism to follow, and not even give you a new doctrine to believe. Rather, my intention is to empower you with the awareness necessary to keep your eyes open as you undertake your journey of evolution, creating your own set of values and beliefs. **I hope that through this new perspective, you will always enable your light to overcome your shadows.** Our society is becoming darker, filled with distractions and the inability for man to realize that his time here is limited, so I hope this light will guide your way.

I should also note that this will most likely be my last piece of literary work, partially because it completes my most important work, and partially because the rest of my work will be focused on bringing these definitions to as many people as I can during my final personality cycle.

As many of you know, I am not an author, but rather a teacher, one whose life purpose has always been to help others find out who they really are, set their own values and beliefs, and become the best versions of themselves. I have always led people who want to lead themselves. This book marks the end of my greatest work and the conclusion that so many have waited for since the birth of *Third Circle Theory* in 2013. While my work as the author ends, my work as the teacher continues throughout the world in the years to come. My commitment to my chosen purpose will never end as it is a piece of my very own reputation to leave behind.

"You live as long as the last person who remembers you."

Introduction:
Boundary: An Established Definition

Truth: What You Choose to Believe

If truth is based on perspective and perspective creates truth, then can one say that only one possible scenario exists to answer a question? One could argue that the same question could have two answers, and both answers could be accurate.

Let's take the simple question of deciding that oranges are orange in color. Is this statement true because of our acceptance that oranges are colored as such? Or because we have come to accept that the word "orange" is associated with a specific color?

In other words, did the fruit determine the connotation of color or vice versa? This structure allows us to give value to language and communicate with a set of words that are commonly accepted as truth. Structure gives us the validation that our perspectives are aligned to an accepted truth and that any variations of these truths are considered mistruths.

While the majority of humans need constant structure to define their perspective, some humans—known as "Higher Humans"—are able to shift their perspectives. They redefine those definitions on an ongoing basis, giving them the ability to push the boundary of their internal belief system.

Most humans live in a box consisting of hard edges, the four boundaries that enable them to slowly make sense of everything happening to them. "Higher Humans" live in circles, understanding that the size of their circle (environment) is constantly changing (expanding and retracting) based on their understanding of this environment. Therefore, they live in a world that is defined by its future possibility, not its past circumstance.

This is what I refer to as "the lack of an absolute truth." Something many simply cannot learn to accept.

"An absolute truth is a personal perspective of choice that a reality you face is the absolute truth and reverting from it could be dangerous, reckless, or simply wrong."

We can attribute simple examples found in the First Circle. Most religious individuals believe their religion or God to be the absolute truth. No matter what evidence or lack of evidence there may be, they will forever choose to believe. We can also look at examples that are much softer, such as one's belief that the formal education system is the only way a person can become successful. While true from one perspective, believing in this from a state of absolute truth means closing the door to any other possibilities and perspectives, giving the person only one way to find success: by going through the formal education system.

On the other hand, higher individuals living in the Third Circle understand that an absolute truth simply cannot exist. They recognize that anything that could hold true in one regard can also be held as false from another's perspective. As a result, your own perspective can be true and false at the same time, both to yourself and others. That **"truth"** is **"choosing to believe something or in something."**

This also leads us to understand that "choice" in itself is based on a similar scale. Delete the idea that a choice is good or bad. Choice, in itself, is a neutral selection. Once we accept the lack of an absolute truth in the context of choice, we remove the need to validate a direction and allow belief to remain our sole guide towards our destination. It no longer becomes the correct path, the correct way to live, or correct direction, but instead simply a step towards our goals or visions.

We must understand that our ability to constantly question our perspective enables us to enhance our self-awareness and, as a result, allow our journey towards self-actualization to be accelerated significantly.

Self-Actualization: A Journey

Self-actualization is an often-misunderstood concept. In Maslow's hierarchy of needs, self-actualization is categorized as the highest level of consciousness a human can achieve. At this level, the individual becomes what we describe as a "Higher Human", but in truth, **being human** in itself **is a boundary that is meant to be transcended.**

The vessel we consider a body as humans is a limitation, a structure for us to use, to be able to make sense of our physical existence and experience on earth.

Our existence consists of our self in the physical and in the subconscious, creating two personas for each and every one of us. We operate by two very different sets of rules. On the physical side, the constraint is the arrow of time (defined as our ability to experience time only at an accepted pace of 60 seconds a minute, and 60 minutes an hour). The other constraint is a reflection of the physical with no restriction of time. Instead, there exists the inability to define a boundary of SELF, therefore never being able to impact a physical world. Our minds cannot decipher between the two and so, for most people, only one specific person exists: one constrained to the arrow of time and the physical world we live in.

As a result, we accept our shape, not by our understanding of ourselves, but rather the reflection of the awareness of others. We project an image on the world. Based on how that image is perceived and accepted by those who see it, we create an image of ourselves. One of confidence, beauty, and strength or perhaps the exact opposite, depending on our perception of this reflection.

Whatever that image we come to accept, it becomes who we are, an accepted "definition" or portrait. In reality, it is how others perceive us. This perception is what we accept as our conceived physical reality, assuming that it is our "self."

This illusion silences the subconscious by preventing us from changing it, especially when it's favorable. Self-actualized individuals possess the capacity to continuously align their vessels and psyche by understanding that all external projections are controlled internally first, enabling them to manipulate what others perceive or the information they receive.

While Maslow defined Self-Actualization as the peak of the performance of being human, I define it as the start of that journey—the beginning of being truly in control of what it means to be human. It isn't the beginning of the end. It's the end of "existing" and the beginning of truly living. It is the stage at which humanity reaches a level of understanding that transcends boundaries of control, absolute truth, a better understanding of time, and, of course, the overcoming of one's internal fears. Achieving self-actualization becomes the freedom that is desired by so many and yet reached by so few.

While becoming a Higher Human requires a person to have self-actualized, this achievement is still far from reaching the level of Higher Human. Self-actualization is the beginning of being a human and having full grasp on your humanity. In other words, every stage of "being" prior to that is the psyche learning to adapt and connect to the boundaries of the vessel.

With practice and with understanding, the psyche's ability to control the vessel is enhanced significantly, giving it the ability to communicate with tools like language, to work outside the boundaries of fear, and gain a deeper understanding of that word "boundary."

The Body: A Vessel

Earlier, I posed a possibility that we are indeed engineered. We can argue about the existence of God, the universe, or a greater force. We are not debating their existence here, but rather understanding that we, as human vessels, have much in common with each other.

We humans are formed in an orderly manner. We have two legs, two feet, two arms, one heart, two lungs, a skeletal system, et cetera. While some of us are defective in nature, the intention is always to end up with a similar product—none of us ever shows a sense of surprise when a baby is born with two eyes, but we feel disappointed when something is not as expected, like a baby missing an arm.

We can even look further than the physical function of a human and say that many of us resemble one another with design characteristics, like similar colored hair, similar colored eyes, and other common features. Even in the areas where we as individuals could be completely different, we still follow a set of possibilities rather than an unlimited and random one. When was the last time you expected a newborn to have purple or pink hair?

Basically, every element of your vessel seems to be made under a set of guidelines, even down to your personality. Think about the concept of astrology, something we are fascinated by. We love to read about our personalities and what's in store for us. Yet, how is it possible that a man-made calendar can accurately decipher that a birthdate dictates specific characteristics or personality traits?

Again, there are too many organized factors of coincidence to argue that being human is indeed a game of randomness, blessing, or God.

Here is where it gets interesting as it pertains to perspective and reflection.

I mentioned earlier that our accepted SELF is an accepted reflection of how others perceive us. Our psyche gives meaning to the information it receives and associates it with values. We, as individuals, also choose to engineer things in the same order and way we ourselves have been engineered. What is a vessel but a carrier of the psyche? Think about the vessel and psyche as physical and metaphysical coming together, body as the carrier and the mind the driver. Let's break down the marvels of transportation (also known as transport vessels) that we as humans have created, then, compare them to our own vessels—specifically, those we have learned to most rely on to enhance our abilities, like moving faster and flying.

I reference the automobile and the airplane as examples.

Let's use the automobile as the reference point, since it is more commonly accepted and used across the globe. More of us use or own cars than airplanes.

The car serves the sole purpose of enabling our motion through time and space to be significantly accelerated over our conventional vessel (the body). While we have many reasons for owning vehicle, the purpose of a vehicle has always been to get a person from one location to another. Even the more expensive vehicles follow that very same purpose, doing the job much faster and with more comfort. While we can argue that not all vehicles are built for speed, we can't argue that every vehicle has indeed gotten faster over time, even those whose focus wasn't based on providing a performance element to begin with. We are simply in this never-ending pursuit of allowing our vessel to travel through time and space at a faster rate than is possible on foot. We can enhance that even further with airplanes.

Now, how are automobiles built?

It is comprised of a frame (skeleton), four tires (four limbs), an engine (a heart) a CPU (a brain), a transmission (nervous system) and more. We can question why the vessels that are man-made are so similar to our own bodies. Next, we go even further and give individualized aspects to such automobiles by adding colors, or features that appeal to each individual person.

We have always created unique vehicles to meet the appeal of an array of consumers, but have we ever attempted to change the order of engineering? Every automotive manufacturer has attempted to make its vehicles faster, but none have attempted to make a modern car without an Electronic Control Unit (the brain of a car) or without a frame. While electric cars may take engines out of cars, I argue that they are not removing engines; they are simply giving the vehicle a new diet that consists of electrical energy, not of fossil fuel. Even electric vehicles, in essence, are obsessed with speed. The only manufacturer that was able to penetrate the EV automotive market did so because of "speed", enabling the masses to adopt the idea faster. Hundreds of previous attempts failed as a result of that very simple component missing from the equation. The purpose of a car as a whole is to enable our bodies to move with higher speeds. If we can understand this perspective, we can see the connection between an automotive vessel and a human vessel on a much greater level than saying, "it's just a car."

The advancement of vessels is also aligned to our understanding of dimensions. We are three-dimensional beings living in a four-dimensional world. Our automobiles are two-dimensional vessels functioning in a three-dimensional world; they are limited in their capacity based on the environment they can travel in, not just in speed. This is why we have created airplanes, to allow us to have better vessel carriers that can do what a car does, but with increased speed.

This evolution is also not random, but rather the organic progression of our understanding of ourselves and our constant pursuit of saving time. But why do we always insist on saving time in everything we do?

Time: Perspective

For the longest time, man has been obsessed with the notion of time—saving time, using time, and understanding time. Scientists have spent their entire lives devoted to understanding time and why it can only move forward. Einstein himself was defined by his understanding of time relativity, giving a perspective that opened the door to space travel today.

In order to understand time, we must understand the value of time in space. First, in what I call "Space Time" but also how dimensions work, especially as they pertain to the first five for now. We will use "string theory" to understand these first five dimensions.

To allow you to understand this concept, I am referencing a paragraph from physlink.com

"String theory is a term used to describe a set of very closely related mathematical models of elementary particles and their interactions. String theories seek to unify the theory of gravity (general relativity) with the three other forces of nature, which we have learned to describe using the techniques of quantum field theory.

In string theory, the known elementary particles are no longer described as dimensionless mathematical point-objects but rather as extended one-dimensional objects (hence the name 'string'). These objects may be either open bits of a line or closed into loops. The size of the individual strings is so fantastically small that any experiment we could possibly perform on an elementary particle would not reveal its string-like nature—it would look just like the point-particle we expect.

Since the strings have a finite size, they can vibrate. All the known particles of nature are just different modes of vibration of the string. Thus, the string is the only truly 'fundamental' particle.

For string theories to be mathematically consistent, they need to describe strings moving in more than four dimensions. If a string theory is the correct theory of nature, these extra dimensions must obviously be hidden from our ability to detect them. The general assumption is that they are 'compact'—rolled into dimension so small that our everyday experience only reveals the four large ones (three space, one time) in which we live."

Let's understand dimensions from the beginning in a simpler manner.

1 Dimension = The ability to exist in a single place in time and space (like a dot)

2 Dimension = The ability to function from A point to B point (like a line)

3 Dimension = The ability to function from A point to B point, with an understanding of a future C point (like a triangle)

4 Dimension = The ability to function with a limitation of Time, not just Space

5 Dimension = The ability to function through verticals of possible times

This simplified explanation allows you to understand our obsession with time, so much so because of our limited understanding of it. Every paradox, every possible scientific equation simply cannot explain anything past the fourth dimension, which is time. Perhaps that results from the lack of evolution and information, or perhaps because this was the intended function of the human vessel, not to beat time, but rather give it meaning.

If we analyze the evolution of humans through the dimensions, then it would make sense, but if we instead understand that dimensions are the parameters of control for the vessels and their functions, we can then associate a certain type of vessel to a certain type of dimension. Once that connection occurs, we start uncovering that the issue is a question of limitation, not understanding.

We can break down this concept even further.

Let's assume all species live simultaneously in a five-dimensional space-time continuum, but we all can only comprehend or experience one dimension ahead of the one we function in. For example, as humans, we experience a fourth-dimensional world (one where time controls everything) but can only function in three dimensions (our ability to control our motion).

While we do experience the fourth dimension, we are bound by its control; we cannot fold time and space; we can only move forward in time through what we refer to as the "arrow of time", which is our understanding of the 24 hours that consist in our day and the pace at which we accept a clock takes us through it. If you were to ask someone to meet you at the local mall, they couldn't comply without knowing "what time" you wanted them to meet you there, and they could not move backwards if they missed the agreed-upon time.

Living in a fourth dimension means that while we have the *ability* to move freely in three dimensions—including up and down—we cannot *give purpose* to our motion without associating it with time.

On the other hand, an animal is a two-dimensional being living in a three-dimensional space. While the animal can freely move to and from points A, B and C, its consciousness doesn't allow it to plan its point C. It must forever travel to point B before discovering the next point. That said, the reason for such straight-line, two-dimensional behaviors is that animals do not have an understanding of time. This differentiates their ability to plan ahead and strategically leverage their usage of space, forcing them to engage in mobility by simply traveling one line at a time from point A to B only. Even though a point C exists in their environment, it only unveils itself once they reach point B. Similar to the human's mobility being limited by time, the animal is limited by its inability to *see* time. Similar constraints, different perspectives.

The interesting element here is that, if species are more than one dimension apart, they simply cannot understand the connection they have to one another. Let's use the example of a snail (a one-dimensional being operating in a two-dimensional world) and a human vessel (a three-dimensional being existing in a four-dimensional world). The pace or speed of existence, as defined by our acceptance of the arrow of time, is so different in these two living things that one cannot acknowledge the existence of the other. We do not need snails for any reason, nor can they make sense of what we are to them; we do not interact with them for any reason.

This separation of time and space creates an interesting perspective as it pertains to "time" and its power. We travel through time and space at a significantly faster pace than a snail, in fact, so significant (8,800 times faster) that we technically could experience that same space continuum 8,800 times while the snail experiences it just one time.

So comes the question, what are we to a snail?

If you were to race the snail for 100 meters, you would be able to complete this race so much faster than the snail that you would have full control over its fate and its ability to finish the race. You could pour water on it, crush it, place a giant set of bricks in its way, and create just about any circumstance for it. Yet, the snail would have no way of understanding why such bizarre events are happening.

As a matter of fact, the snail may not even comprehend your interference and would place a value of randomness or faith on the events (if it had consciousness, of course). This occurs simply because of the human's ability to control the time-space continuum of the snail by applying significantly faster pace or motion through that set of time.

Which brings us to the next question:

If we can terminate the snail's life, if we can position the snail in time and space or change the snail's circumstance without its own knowledge and the snail cannot even see us due to our size, are we therefore considered God to the snail?

That brings forth the uncomfortable question: What if a species living in a fifth dimension holds the same fate over our existence similar to the fate that we hold over the snail? We often label acts as "not meant to be" or "it was fate" or even identify "how we caused such anomalies like the power of manifestation." While one perspective suggests that everything in the universe is random, another perspective could be explained by the manipulation/interference of a higher dimension life-force or entity.

So, in order to explain the possible interference that we *receive*, we must understand the interference we *create*. The reason we are able to play God with the snail is because of our ability to manipulate its understanding or lack of understanding of time. Our ability to function in a state that occurs 8,800 times faster than the snail enables us to control its lifeline, to see and create its future, and even trace its past—all on the simple basis that we can occupy the same space while functioning at a significantly higher speed.

We can only assume that, if another species experienced time at such a significant advantage over us, it could also hold the same power over our time-space continuum. This brings me back once more to our human limitations to the arrow of time, and our ability to experience in one forward motion. A beginning and an end to an event or life is based on a straight-line theory (two-dimensional), but yet we exist and experience life in a four-dimensional world.

While the majority of humans experience and live life in a four-dimensional world, their thinking is limited to a two-dimensional one, one where everything is defined by right or wrong, by beginning and ending, and by a continuous desire to establish an absolute truth for themselves.

This inability to look or perceive the world from a four-dimensional space prevents the expansion of the psyche and instead limits its expansion to the boundaries of the vessel. In a simpler way, a human is incapable of driving anywhere a road doesn't exist on the sole fear that you would get lost.

So, if a basic, unconscious human lives in a two-dimensional world, then he can only comprehend his next move, but if one lives in a three-dimensional world, he can comprehend the possibilities of his next moves while still within the boundaries of what he defines as a beginning or ending.

Further, it is only when a human self-actualizes that he gains an interesting understanding of time. They no longer see that time has a beginning or ending. Instead, they perceive that time is continuously expanding and retracting, understanding that every action leads to millions of possible outcomes, and that every outcome can create an alternative future, one that has already taken place to other five-dimensional beings, and yet hasn't been experienced by ourselves.

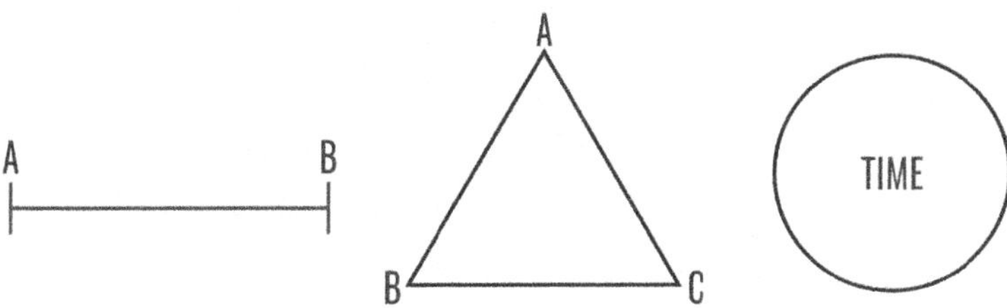

Time can therefore be manipulated as you understand that there is no past, present and future. You comprehend instead that **one's ability to travel in time isn't defined by their ability to change the past but** to understand that **the present we are currently experiencing is the past and future simultaneously.**

"Time and space have always been one and existed in their entirety at once, not going from a beginning to an ending but rather expanding and retracting."

Our experience of time is extremely limited as we are only able to experience it through our vessel (which is bound to experiencing it 60 seconds at a time through the arrow of time). The vessel gives meaning to the psyche, enabling it to give a beginning and ending value to its existence, and thus forcing the psyche to evolve in a limited time within controlled guidelines. One could call this a "lifecycle." I would call this meaning the "boundary of evolution." Such a boundary allows the psyche to understand time and make sense of it, so it doesn't lose itself as it attempts to connect time and space without a boundary set on how to navigate it.

What is a clock but an engineered boundary of time?

What is a vessel but a boundary of the psyche?

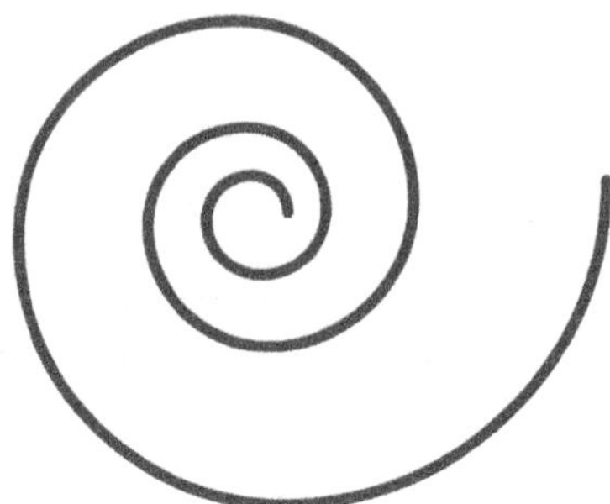

Since a beginning and end is necessary for most humans to make sense of their purpose and existence, I will use the same boundary of control to help you understand the journey of the psyche from the birth of the vessel to its arrival at the gate of choice.

So, if time already exists and our experience of it is delayed, then it is possible that our future has not been pre-determined or written but rather has already taken place in the universe. Therefore, we as humans are simply experiencing time at our own pace, based on our limited level of third-dimensional consciousness. Later in the book, I will break down this concept I refer to as “Destiny Theory”, showing you exactly how your own lifecycle has already been pre-written by no one other than yourself. I will also demonstrate how you are now only experiencing your own timeline, one second at a time forward. This theory not only explains “déjà vu” but also means that as larger timelines expand or interfere in ours, changes can occur that we least expect or understand, which would bring up the ultimate question:

Knowing you have already made your choices, taken your directions, established your limitations and defined your purpose and are now simply experiencing the accumulation of such choices, would you still live your life as you have chosen to so far?

Life: Choice of Perspective

I am going to walk you through a few definitions that will help shape your perspective around choice so that you can easily overcome circumstance in your life. This perspective impacts everything from your understanding of how energy gets distributed to how we as humans can make sense of connecting our choice of purpose to our day-to-day activities.

First, let's break down energy.

In *Third Circle Theory*, I broke down the evolution of the human mind as it becomes more aware of itself. I guided you along the mind's journey to discovering itself through circumstance, society, and finally reaching the beginning of its self-awareness journey by mastering life. **While circumstance has and always will be man's greatest challenge to finding himself, society will always remain his most treacherous one.** One's mastery of circumstance requires the ability to overcome one's own expansion, while the mastery of society requires the ability to overcome and navigate other people's expansion as it pertains to you.

One of the greatest misconceptions has been that the journey from one circle to the next (as explained in *Third Circle Theory*) is linear, like a straight line. That suggests living in one circle and moving on to the next. It is this need for a beginning and ending that leads humans to wanting to seek answers in such a manner as described in the graphic below.

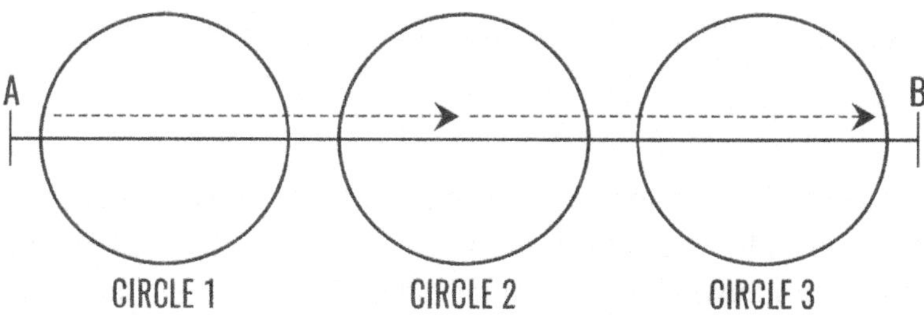

However, in order to understand growth, we must change our perspective once more on how the journey takes place. We should no longer seek neither a beginning nor an ending. Instead, **we must seek a state of being for today, and a state of becoming for tomorrow—one where we do not move forward but *expand* into the person we wish to become.** Travelling in a linear manner, no matter where your destination is, references one's ability to leave where they exist in time and space and reappear where they want to be. We must move from point A to point B, which means that we are technically leaving behind who we are. Now, if we look at expansion as *the mechanism for growth, not travel*, then we realize that we never left point A. Instead, we *absorbed* all aspects of life from point A to B without ever leaving. Expansion is an important concept as **the line that connects two points is two-dimensional in nature while the circle that expands into absorbing multiple points becomes four-dimensional.**

When we visualize this as a graphic, then you can clearly see that the growth from an expansion is inclusive, while the growth from a forward motion is limiting and dismissive.

This concept of expansion (as seen in the graphic above) versus forward motion is essential to understand. We as humans are used to creating boundaries around our understanding of life. Boxes that we have come to accept as control mechanisms are such boundaries.

We fail to realize that a circle cannot expand in a box, but boxes can be controlled within a circle. This is the core essence of why so many of us have limited perspective and limited understanding of circumstance, society, and life. In the simplest form, **we must understand and manage the boundaries of control within our lives, rather than be defined by them.**

Boundaries of control are our consciousness giving structure to our vessel, but our inability to decipher between control and the vessel forces us to stay trapped within such confines and, in some cases, never escape.

A simple example of this would be religion. While there is perhaps necessary structure and good baseline of behavior in just about every religion, many people cannot operate outside the guideline of their beliefs. They cannot look at religion as a means of established structure, but rather as an absolute truth.

A box that creates a boundary of control is necessary in order to function. Look at venturing outside of this boundary as betrayal rather than evolution. In simplest terms, define that inside the box is right and outside the box is wrong.

The same example can be applied to a conservative mind that has accepted the societal trap set for him with the formal education system. While there is necessary structure and good baseline for behavior in the idea of formal education, many students cannot understand that its role is to establish a *baseline*, not a *destination*. As a result, many students do not understand that their success isn't directly correlated to their degree. Instead, they look at this scenario from an absolute perspective—one where staying in school is the only way to find success while leaving leads to failure.

Boundaries of control—or these so-called boxes—are structures created to enable the constant motion of people through time, preventing them from staying stuck in any single time/space continuum. In education, we have progression by having grades and classes of various levels. In Corporate America, we receive promotions that prevent us from growing past the control mechanisms. Think about it: We work within a box (position) and get good at it. We then become more aware and start to wonder "what if...?". We are then immediately promoted to a larger box where we can expand more. This form of controlled expansion allows us to stay within the boxes we have been assigned but gives us a sense of falsified growth—one where we believe we are advancing when, in reality, we are simply given a larger cage that we haven't yet outgrown.

While this concept of being caged may seem dark and unpleasant, it is a necessity to growth. It is easier for us to grow within cages than it is to roam free without structure. Imagine if we had no roads to drive on when going to work. With no structure or direction, our drives anywhere would take so much effort that we would end up wasting a lot of our time doing something that has no meaning. As a result, we would be prevented from working on more important tasks.

Structure is needed, but the issue isn't the structure we need to grow, but rather that we find a level of comfort with having others set such structures for us so that we never outgrow them. Our parents set structures for us while we are growing up. Many children end up continuously waiting for instructions even in their twenties and beyond, unable to know what to do or how to do it. They shift the boundaries of control from parents to teachers to supervisors, never really expanding past the box where they have become comfortable.

We treat animals in this very same manner. Think about a hamster or cat. We leave them in cages or in our homes, expecting them to obey our commands and that expectation comes from the idea that we are the ones feeding them and taking care of them. Their obedience comes from the guarantee that, by staying within the four walls we have created for them, they will receive their rewards (food) and survive. When the door is open for them to leave and be free, they often stay inside these confines, rethinking their need to explore past those created boundaries. We often recognize this fear and leverage it to ensure their obedience increases over time. While we understand this behavior to be their function and their weakness, we as individuals fall victim to the same behavior in our own control mechanisms at work, home, or school. We stay confined to the same cage as those we cage and for the exact same reasons.

While we can argue that this is simply one aspect of life, we can also see this from another perspective, one related to our dimensional understanding. I mentioned earlier that animals are two-dimensional beings and that humans are four-dimensional beings. While the animal has an excuse for his behavior, the human does not, because of his understanding of time.

The animal doesn't understand its life span and has no consciousness towards the journey, only its own ability to constantly travel from point A to point B. This is part of the reason that its survival is its priority, not its growth. It has no ability to understand the concept of expansion.

You do.

Yet, in many instances, you are more concerned about securing your survival than expanding into your growth. One of the main reasons people go towards the Dreamer Stage of the First Circle is that their expansion through time is happening outside of their control. The arrow of time only moves forward. However, their expansion in space isn't taking place because of their commitment to survival.

As a result, time passes and expands, but the individual doesn't, giving them a feeling of having been left behind. The animal would never care because while it occupies space, it doesn't have a timeline and, therefore, doesn't have a sense for missed time. But you do.

Understanding expansion means understanding that the goal of life isn't to travel from point A to Point B and so on (as that is two-dimensional thinking), but rather to fold time by expanding yourself to be Point A *and* Point B at the same exact time (four-dimensional behavior). You are then able to embrace the experience that comes with such expansion, rather than simply be at a different point of space at a different time.

While most people understand that they must expand their energy, they also believe that we are the source of the energy we expand. In reality, that energy already exists with or without us. **As Higher Humans, our goal should not be to create energy and allow it to expand inwards or outwards, but rather to understand how to channel it through us** and allow it to expand, leveraging us as the channel.

This enables us to tap into energy on demand, rather than trying to create a new energy flow from the point of creation to the point of destruction. Once more, this need to let go of a beginning and ending. Instead, *learn to be the flow itself*, the experience or the middle of the equation, per se. A simple example would be the understanding of finance in society. It is much better to understand the entire spectrum of cash flow rather than just to focus on how much money you would like to make. It's about the equations of life more than the results of those equations.

Once you truly comprehend this idea of expansion and retraction, you start to realize why living in the boxes set forth for you can become dangerous to your ability to grow. Boxes control energy while circles expand and retract freely.

So why do such boxes exist?

In the simplest of thoughts, the boxes that frame our perspective today have been created and formed by individuals who were indeed Higher Humans. We may look at such control mechanisms as manipulative and wonder why people who are more in touch with them want others to be confined to such boundaries. However, we would be asking the wrong question.

While the box of your thoughts can be looked at as a boundary, it can also be viewed as a form of structural learning. It is very difficult for a human to make sense of things when the structure of them is constantly expanding and retracting. Firm and control-based smaller boxes can help each and every one of us play closer attention to how to function within each.

Commitment: A Path to Creativity

If our goal is not to stay trapped in such boxes, then we must question the purpose of such boxes and structures. The ultimate goal of the human body is to assign itself a purpose, so that it can free itself of its own boundary. While purpose has a lot to do with the progress one makes toward actualization, it isn't relevant to such boundaries of control. This is partially because **purpose is the initiation of one's choice to turn their thoughts from boundaries to expansion.**

Boxes or boundaries do, however, hold a purpose. They give birth to the vessel's ability to practice a state of mind called "excellence". One of the driving forces that enables the spirit to gain confidence in its own self-image is the ability to move from a state of discovery to a state of excellence. This motion allows the success of the behavior to reward the belief in the journey and give man even more confidence towards eventually forming his own boundary rather than be given one.

Consider it from this perspective: If man lacks confidence or doesn't understand how to project confidence, and he roams freely in a city in order to meet a mate, he will feel lost. He will make efforts at multiple locations, losing a point of focus. This man fails to realize that he is not compounding his efforts, causing additional barriers of doubt to cast over his mind.

What if he is in the wrong location to meet people? What if he is there at the wrong time? What if he is wearing the wrong outfit? And so many more factors. These questions will push him to overcome his own doubts and fears multiple times with each and every interaction, instead of building confidence with each barrier he encounters and use such experience to become more capable by the next one he encounters.

However, by creating a control mechanism for himself and choosing to go to one specific bar for an entire week, he is then able to focus on the task at hand and not every circumstance leading to the task. By being in one single location, he is able to compound data he is receiving or gathering—understanding other's behaviors, how to dress, how to interact—and also creating a familiar feeling for himself.

He no longer fears his ability to fit into his environment. He shifts his focus to the task itself. With each interaction comes improvement. Improvement focused on one task is much more likely to bring a sense of excellence to the mind that is in charge of it. When we commit to excellence, we notice a pattern of success that is bound to bring more confidence in ourselves, once more shaping a very different image of our own being and others.

We can use a similar example in the boundaries of structure created for you at work. In most cases, we seek jobs because we lack skills, and have yet to master or commit to any specific form or skill. We choose to go into a structured opportunity (even if subconscious in nature) in order to identify an opportunity to be part of something. Since we do not know where we fit, we select a profession based on our external skills, or lack thereof.

We do so because it is easier to practice one skill in one position rather than to figure everything out from the beginning. Your work within an organization is often based on one role or one position. While you may undertake more, the structure is often unilateral, like salesman or receptionist. Each role is clearly defined with a specific set of tasks, goals, and structure of operation. The more you practice the role, the better you become in it.

While your skills improve, you are given an opportunity at excellence within the role. As I mentioned earlier, once you find a strong enough level of success practicing in one box, a new one is offered to you (promotion), which leads you to working in the next box and taking on more. No matter the size of your box, it remains your box as other people will be in charge now of your previous boxes.

Many of you may look at this as a form of manipulation or control, no different than those of you who believe that "we are paid to build other people's dreams". In reality, we work for ourselves, and none of us would work a job without a wage associated with it. None of us choose to work at a fast food chain because we believe in the work they are doing. We work there, trading our hours for a wage we accept, and we believe this job to be our best option at the time. Our lack of commitment to excellence and ourselves is what keeps us there.

Nonetheless, working *in* an organization rather than *on* one is much easier. The definition of your role, its expectations, and its direction are not in your hands, forcing you to focus on the task and the task alone. Similar to being lost in a city seeking the right bar, we are confined to just one bar (the company) and given just one task (the job). Once again, this situation allows us to gain confidence in our skills and abilities while limiting the external factors that can hinder our growth. Building a business is the exact opposite. While the person may be a successful plumber, he needs to factor in everything—being a great marketer, salesman, accountant and money manager—before he can practice the art of plumbing. This requirement makes him less likely to find a sense of excellence at the same speed or timeframe as the one who is given the tools and boxed structure to only practice plumbing under another company's name.

Similar to the way that corporations force the compartmentalizing of such skills, we must learn to do the same for our growth. We must focus on each step to the point of excellence or mastery.

Mastery and commitment to excellence with those boxes in our lives are what enables us to wonder "what if" which leads us to a conscious choice of stepping outside the boxes. Van Gogh had to learn and master the rules of how to paint in order to become skilled enough to paint things people hadn't seen or in ways people hadn't thought of. While creativity is what enabled him to be recognized today as one of the most powerful Expressionists of our era, it was excellence that led him to finding the confidence to undertake such creativity.

Mastery of any skill or function leads to the overall confidence in one's ability and the pursuit of excellence as a habit, leading to the birth of belief.

Most people seek to believe in something in life and to be given a sense of purpose or destination. However, most of them do not take into consideration that **believing in one's self is the first step to committing to excellence** as a philosophy of life, not just on a task. When one embraces this simple but difficult task, one finds that direction and purpose are a choice, not simply given to you by a higher power.

Purpose in itself is commitment to choice of belief at any given time. The choice to commit to excellence pertains to the space we occupy. In simpler words, purpose is your choice of what you commit to at various stages of your life. You can find purpose in being a cashier at a supermarket as much as you can find purpose by helping feed the poor in third world countries. **When we choose our roles consciously, we assign ourselves purpose. When we assign ourselves purpose, we commit to excellence in our practice of such purpose.** Purpose isn't constant. Purpose is evolving and an extension of yourself that is no different than the boxes of structure you live in. If your box is a square, then your purpose is limited, but if you understand how to change in order to free yourself of the absolute truths that created such structures, then your purpose will also expand with you.

BOX + Excellence = Creativity = Transformation of Box into Circle

Business: An Expression of Creativity

When you look at the confines of a box, and realize that its purpose is to create structure, you also realize that structure in itself can hinder creativity. Structure gives you a clear path of operation rather than enabling you to be creative in your approach. The commitment to excellence is a powerful outcome that can come easier should the focal point in itself be within a box. It can also be met in limitation if that commitment isn't from a chosen subject but rather one that is assigned.

For the longest time, we as a society have praised the work of today's wealthiest businessmen, individuals whose businesses cater to the masses who consume their products and services daily. They remain relevant because of their wealth or generational fortunes, which acts as a reminder of what others should aspire to work for. As a society however, we are starting to forget the real innovators who mattered, those whose leadership we should be following, those who have enabled us to witness a level of creativity higher than the average man and whose expressions of creativity have led the way to what real entrepreneurship is.

In *Third Circle Theory*, I identified such men as the Higher Men, the individuals—like Walt Disney, Henry Ford, Nikola Tesla, Vincent Van Gogh, Hans Zimmer, and Christopher Nolan—whose life's work would transcend their mortal life. Individuals living or dead who understood that entrepreneurship wasn't just about the execution of a successful business model but one's ability to show the world a new perspective or create social change through creativity.

We must understand that while business may seem to be a means of abundance and the creation of wealth, it is a vehicle meant to deliver creativity to others. Entrepreneurship, in itself, is the art of such creation. Business today doesn't have to be entrepreneurial in nature, but it is then a facilitation of the boundaries that confine us.

For man to rise and break free of such boundaries, he must understand the separation of business and entrepreneurship. He must understand that while business facilitates a delivery and can exist both within and without a box, entrepreneurship is the only path for the creative genius. that man is to manifest itself. Entrepreneurship, even if unsuccessful in reaching the masses, will always remain an imprint on the world we live in.

Van Gogh, Picasso, and other artists of the past may not have experienced much monetary success in their lifetimes, but the imprint of their work has forever changed the landscape of inspiration for others to follow. Furthermore, while they never enjoyed the fruits of their work from a societal standpoint, their intentions were never to sell art but rather to bring their view of the world for others to see.

A true expression of creativity is not bound by the acceptance or understanding of society at the time of its presentation but rather an opportunity to shape a future perspective that has yet to be accepted or understood.

Creativity: A Path to Immortality

Creativity is the component in the human journey that enables man to find his place, his purpose, his voice, and his identity. Creativity enables him to transcend his existence and mortality. This evolution is the most powerful and final step towards self-actualization, a stage not focused on the end of one's journey, but rather the beginning and birth of the higher man within each of us.

Creative geniuses, also known as the higher man, are individuals who give birth to new perspective, new advancement, and new direction. It is within their vision that the future of mankind gets decided and the balance of life restored. While you may question if each individual should or shouldn't be an entrepreneur in their lifetime, you should also consider that entrepreneurship is the expression of one's creativity and giving birth to the creative genius within and therefore must be looked at as such, rather than just a path to abundance and wealth in the context of the psyche, not the vessel.

The connection of such creativity on a surface level becomes a business. That, in itself, is very much connected to the abundance we have come to expect once society acknowledges our creative efforts. Similar to our perspective of time, our thoughts towards creativity must be broken down to follow our existence in our dimensions. Creativity is a four-dimensional manifestation that transcends time, but a business is a three-dimensional concept. This difference is why creativity (entrepreneurship) transcends our vessel's existence but building a business ends with our vessel's demise.

Yet, **the Higher Man and the creative genius** I speak of becoming **are slowly becoming an extinct breed and being replaced by the last man, a by-product of the herd mentality that has plagued this world for the last century.**

The Last Man no longer aspires for greatness and no longer seeks to shape his own circle. Rather, he finds himself content to be belonging to other people's prisons and boundaries for the sake of survival. A man who has lost the desire to create has lost the passion for excellence and instead has found himself to be complacent and accepting of his own behavior. No longer pushing to find his own truth but rather controlled by the perspective of others. One commonly accepted, tormented by the need to belong and without aspiration.

Understanding this allows us to enter the realm of the higher man with aspiration, clarity and a deeper acceptance that, regardless of our chosen purpose in this lifetime, it is our creative effort that enables us to find our personal sense of truth—a truth based not on a beginning or ending, not based on an absolute right or wrong, but rather based on the simplicity of the dimensional perspective we retain. Understanding that, as four-dimensional beings, **we do not have control of time but rather control our function within it.** The function of choosing a purpose, and committing to its progress, therefore, give our life meaning.

Section 1:
The Prisoner, The Creator, The Master

PART I: The Prisoner

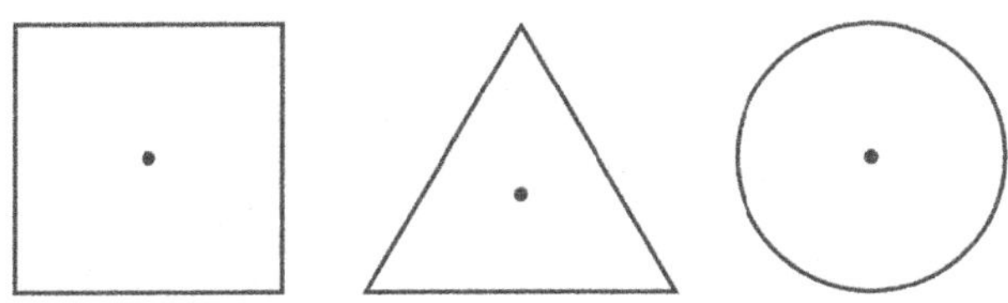

Prison: The Inability to Unite the Personality and the SELF

In my 20+ years in business and 38 years on this planet, I have come to understand that humanity is indeed divided into three distinct types of humans.

As the prophet Zarathustra said in his earlier teachings—followed by famous philosopher Nietzsche in his masterpiece "Thus Spoke Zarathustra" —each person can be classified into one of three categories: The Herd, The Last Man, or the Higher Man.

These three categories aren't based on social status, wealth, religion, or race, but rather the state of evolution and acceptance one falls into.

Digging into this information may come a with a sense of discomfort. Those without a clear path to a higher state of being will often reject new information and perspective. Instead, they justify their basis for their lack of evolution. This is the same as telling someone they are poor, and, while factual in context of the universal acceptance of wealth or poverty, one would argue as to why their situation exists as is, rather than to accept their current reality and strive for a better one.

This level of deflection doesn't come from internal denial but by the idea of a limited belief system founded in a three-dimensional world. This perspective is backed by an inability to see the road or path to get out of such situation, which gives birth to what we call the "Herd Mentality".

Those in the Herd cannot find a destination worth pursuing, or a purpose they choose to commit to. They also find it very easy to convince others to join their state of acceptance of their own immobility in life. The Herd members remind others of the dangers of attempting greatness and failing. They often remind others of the ease of the Herd's benefit: life without materialism or competition, and a life not lived in mastery but through the control of a master.

The Last Man on the other hand, is still a member of the herd in its complacency and enjoyment of all the control mechanisms. This individual strives for a master, but puzzles over the possibilities of the other side. The Last Man will have tendencies to strive but only within the boundaries of the control mechanisms it can understand. He is excited by entertainment and technology but living in a world where survival and happiness become the central focus of a lifetime. Gifted with intelligence and awareness the

Last Man lacks in belief, self-awareness and the ability to operate within a four-dimensional space confined by time, without a master.

The Higher Man on the other hand—also referred to, as the creative genius—is one who understands the correlation of the arrow of time with his existence. He strives for excellence on a daily basis and values the power of creativity. The Last Man gives his life purpose through the meaning of progress and continues to follow through with his aspirations

Mastery: Renouncing a Master

There was a time when man was the by-product of his aspiration. He sought the ability to transcend himself, living in a state of greatness and possibility, pushing the envelope of mastery. Today, man has been domesticated, living a life built with the boundaries established for him by others. He is entertained by meaningless technologies and concepts and has given up the idea of breaking free of his own limitations, giving himself not to mastery of his highest hopes and aspirations but to the comforts of a master.

What is a master but one who takes away our choice in exchange for stability and peace within the boundary of their control mechanisms, chaining us to a two-dimensional idea, no different than how we domesticate animals? While one may make the argument that we create boundaries of controls for animals as they have been set for us, one cannot argue that animals, unlike humans, do not have an understanding of time and give in unconsciously; however, **when man gives in to a master, he gives up his control of time, his aspirations, and his beliefs, which are his greatest gifts.**

He gives up his dimensional rite of passage, one where in exchange for safety and shelter he will put down his arrow and no longer aspire for greatness but rather aspire to serve.

In *The Gate of Choice*, we will break down the most important philosophies of life that enable us to go from a state of being controlled by masters to a state of personal mastery. This transformation is especially important to one's ability to regain control over their dimensional alignment.

We can break this process down into three basic steps:

- The first step is to overcome the control mechanisms that force man to stay committed to a master rather than mastery itself.
- The second step is the ability to awaken the creative genius within and reach a higher level of aspiration.
- The third step is the ability to surrender the SELF to a state of conscious choice.

Through this progressive journey, the vessel can be mastered to a state of higher vibration that leads to a stronger connection to the SELF and the ability to live in a state of continuous consciousness. At this point, he is finally able to face the Gate of Choice—a gate at which man must ensure his personality is aligned to the final personality he wishes to keep. At this point, he is no longer confined to his vessel but rather evolves to a true four-dimensional being.

Personality: The Overcoming of EGO

The first step is overcoming the control mechanisms that define our limitations.

When man enters the physical realm, he is given a vessel (which is two-dimensional). As man evolves from child to adulthood, he is not only growing in age, but also grows with the opportunity to evolve his awareness of how to control the vessel by adding an understanding of time. This knowledge enables three-dimensional thinking and motion. Unfortunately, while man continues this evolutionary journey, he finds himself stuck in the realm of living in a four-dimensional world bound by the arrow of time and subject to three-dimensional motion.

The question we attempt to answer isn't "Why?", but rather "How can man break free of such a stagnant path that he finds himself stuck in?" One can attribute much of this to what we call the preset boundaries of control and the need for a master rather than the search for mastery.

From the birth of a vessel to the end of its ability to create, man forms what we call a "personality". The purpose of this personality is to help give the psyche meaning. Enable it to understand how to function in the physical and allow it to form a sense of purpose so that it can eventually return to the source with a forged personality (one of its own choosing), rather than one influenced by the boundaries of control of others.

Boundaries of control are mechanisms created from our environment with the intention to give us structure and direction. While the argument of their positive or negative effects can go on forever, you will learn why such effects are only acceptance of your reality of what you perceive as truth, rather than factual on any level.

The important factor to understand are the words "structure" and "direction" in order to understand the purpose of such boundaries.

Man seeks structure when he doesn't know how to focus; he seeks direction when he doesn't know how to leverage his skills or lack of skills to move towards a set goal. These two basic concepts reflect that a boundary of control is simply there to help us gain focus and skills in order to keep evolving.

The issue as to why we choose to remain under such influences is that the confidence is deflected from the SELF and instead pushed on to the control mechanism itself. Once we gain structure and direction, we do not gain the confidence in our ability to focus and the skills acquired, but rather in the structure and direction given.

In other words, **we place our trust in the process rather than in ourselves.**

Boundaries of control are necessary to allow growth to take place on a physical and psyche level. Unfortunately, they can also become prisons of the mind because while we are thrown into our first boundaries of control (like education, or religion)—often by our loved ones, parents or influential figures—we choose to stay in them based on our fears. **We focus on saving and protecting what we have learned rather than growing to the next phase.**

This can be translated into simple examples focused around those who so deeply fear being poor that they become frugal and live an average life deprived of any pleasure versus those who aren't afraid to risk their savings to progress to a higher level of enjoyment. It's the basis of the fear mindset versus the abundance mindset. While this section has no correlation to money, we can link many of the decisions around money to this, simply because man controls or is controlled by his money and therefore money is an extension of your choices.

When we accept to be bound to such structures, we also allow those in control of them to be our masters and guides through our journey, never really forming our own personality, but rather adopting their boundaries of control for us.

The purpose of every vessel is to help man form a personality; this personality is adopted based on the beliefs, actions, and awareness that man achieves in his lifecycle, according to the boundary of time. At each reset point (known as physical death), we are given an opportunity to choose. We can either occupy a new vessel consciously or unconsciously or choose to keep our established personality moving forward, one where a vessel is no longer required. If the choice happens unconsciously—based on fear or the lack of personality—we are given an opportunity to renew a personality and try again. A personality is how we choose to express our psyche through our vessel. It is especially important to understand this because the personality we choose will never really end, per se, but rather continuously play ping pong between our internal belief and external EGO. Think about it in this graph format.

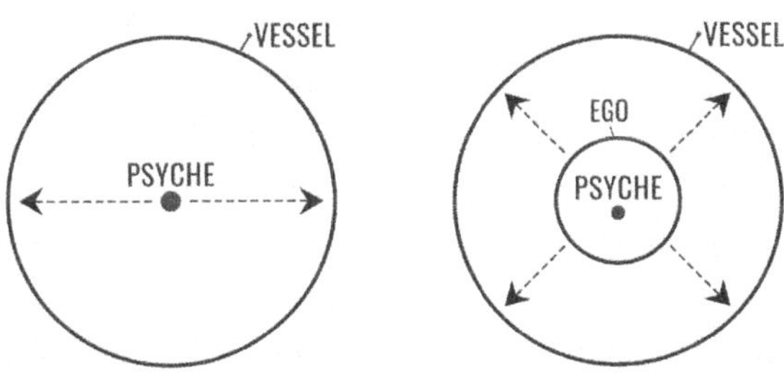

The personality is expressed through the vessel and formed at the core of who we are. Its reflections, however, are sent back to the SELF. When these reflections are misaligned with the information that was once sent to begin with, a new version of our self is created. This is known as "the EGO". Consider the EGO as the defense mechanism that prevents the psyche from being damaged by a reflection of something you are not. So, the EGO is formed; the flow of who we are and our personality is now hindered by this protection mechanism that prevents the flow of thoughts to and from the vessel without interference. **The EGO is often formed to create a sense of importance for the SELF, when the SELF cannot link itself to meaning.** Since a falsified sense of self is created, the psyche no longer has to search for meaning because it has artificially accepted that which it is presented with.

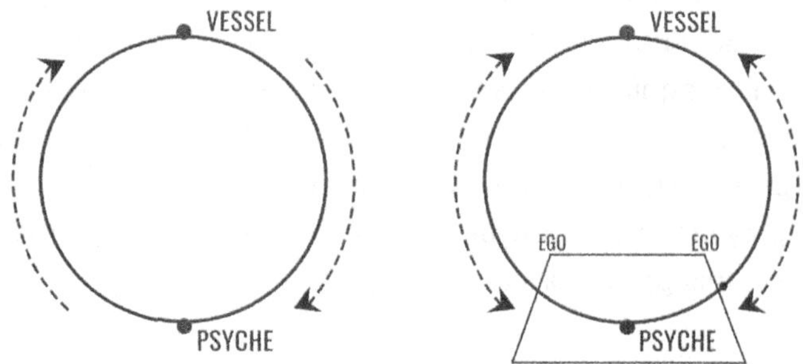

The EGO is the boundary mechanism that traps our psyche, no different than mental boundaries, like fear, trap our vessel. The risk in carrying an EGO during the journey is that it won't allow the personality to truly forge itself but rather fools the personality into accepting its filtered reality.

Those who typically stay stuck develop a stronger EGO and remain fixed in a state of paralysis and conformity. They give up the ability to evolve their personality, which leaves them confined in two prisons simultaneously: one of the mind and one of the EGO, resulting in despair.

To break free of this despair and never-ending loop and to survive one's own mind and personality, one finds refuge under masters. Here, life becomes meaningless and easier to deal with when one no longer has to seek meaning, ultimately finding oneself voluntarily walking into the herd.

One of the largest issues that comes with remaining confined in a boundary of control is that you are not the only one. You will meet others and attract others who are also "stuck" in that same mental state. Unfortunately, these others may even have been there longer than you and have now accepted that such a mental space is where they belong. This state of acceptance, according to renowned philosopher Friedrich Nietzsche, is known as being part of "the herd."

The Herd: A Prison for Mediocrity

The herd, as Nietzsche described it, is the settlement of man, where he no longer aspires for greatness but rather accepts his own fate as destiny.

In "*The Will to Power*," Nietzsche wrote, "Herd Morality is the Danger of dangers, because of its ability to seduce those anxious and fearful in the face of the uncertainty and isolation associated with striving for greatness. In the confusion of their development longing to rest for themselves for once, so as to be free from what oppresses them. Herd Morality acts as a siren's voice, which offers the potential Higher Man a way to escape from his burden's fate into the comfort of mediocrity and emersion in the mass. If Herd Morality becomes too effective in bringing down all that is higher and extraordinary, Nihilism will creep over the world."

This extremely dangerous standard for belonging is the reason many must make sure to break free of the boundaries that chain us to masters. Those who choose this state of being over the state of greatness find themselves becoming that Siren's voice that Nietzsche described.

The Herd Mentality is the enemy of progress. It is the voice that self-sabotages your mind to think "you do not deserve something" and it **is the voice that reminds you that staying a slave to your circumstance is acceptable as long as you are happy.** We as individuals are often taught at a young age to seek happiness—to live a life for the quest of peace, acceptance, love and happiness. We are rarely reminded of the dangers of following such a path for a long duration of time. Staying a slave to a boundary too long will result in our lack of capacity for growth and the birth of what I called the "Settler" in *Third Circle Theory*:

A person whose ambitions and aspiration become forgotten in exchange for comfort.

Man must learn to live dangerously, learn to let go of his fears of failure. He must continuously push for aspiration and greatness and learn to face his despair. The Herd's voice will only get louder, trapping those who give in. To escape the potential hook the Herd can have over our minds, we must learn from a young age to adjust our perspective of possibilities, belief, and, of course, personality aimed at achieving and growing rather than seeking the comfort of life and making happiness our goal.

The personality we must adopt from a young age comes from the basic choice of accepting our place in the world—not as a circumstance, but rather as the starting line. Most will find that life has an imbalance. We struggle to keep up with why we have been given a disadvantage to start, while others will accept that life has given them an opportunity to create a personality that is based on the overcoming of such tasks as the beginning step towards their lives.

The difficulty of such acceptance comes with the pain and emotional strain that must be overcome at an age when perhaps we have yet to experience the opportunity to practice disconnecting our emotions from ourselves.

Emotion in the human vessel is the buffer between the psyche (fourth dimension) and the vessel (third dimension). The greater the emotional reaction, the less connected the two are, creating a constant state of conflict. The longer the conflict, the more likely the EGO manifests itself to create a resolution. This is one of the reasons that people create boundaries of control (protection, or so they think). These boundaries enable them to bury early trauma down to their core and prevent it from ruining their lives. Yet, they never find full freedom from it and instead live a life filled with limitation and fear.

For us to completely break free of the possibility of being lured into the Herd early on, we must disconnect our emotional need to belong with others for safety. We must also discover our own way to create a safe shelter for the SELF to continue growing without a blockage from the EGO.

Let go of trauma as it comes, rather than feel like a victim of our circumstance. One way to accomplish this is to simply let go of the absolute truth (discussed later on). We must understand that the world does not revolve around one person (the SELF) or one personality but that we are the collective power—just one of the pieces that completes the puzzle of life. By letting go of this idea of mattering and removing emotional attachment to the word "I", we can return to a state where mastery is the sole focus, where masters are used to progress rather than to be obeyed. This allows the person to start on their journey of becoming the Higher Man. Now we are faced with the idea of breaking free of the societal traps established to once more chain ourselves to obedience through our evolutionary process.

Society: A Formalized State of Obedience

Society plays a significant role in the evolution of man—partly because man is tied to existing within society, no matter how much he hates it or disagrees with it, and partly because many of the boundaries of control established for man are created from a societal baseline.

We discussed earlier the power of environment on the boundaries of control it creates for man. Think about society as the cage within your environment that doesn't look like a cage. I gave you an earlier example of the hamster who is in a cage but doesn't feel caged until he no longer has his survival accounted for.

Mankind is no different. We are all voluntarily caged until we realize that our survival no longer is accounted for. We go to school only because we are promised a better future as a result of obtaining a degree. We voluntarily go to college and even accept a huge amount of financial burden to do so, but then we feel cheated and caged after we discover that obtaining a degree did not take us where we were promised. We also participate in elections in hopes that politicians we elect will follow our orders, but once we've elected them, we realize that no such direction takes course and once more we feel caged and cheated. Finally, the same behavior continues as we attain employment, being told we matter and the work we do is powerful and important. We continue to devote extra hours and go the extra mile. When we are disposed of because of a mistake or disagreement, we are reminded that our survival is at stake and therefore feel cheated.

The issue with such reminders is that **we feel cheated, when in reality, we simply cheated ourselves by blindly believing a master rather than focusing on mastery.** We cannot take self-accountability in this stage of life. We often reflect our anger and disassociation with a system whose intention was never to help us *succeed* but help us *survive*. This disassociation leads humans to reject the boundaries of control that form a society. Such rejection leads to an inner rebellion that once again keeps us even more trapped.

By rejecting society, we choose to not participate in the game of mastery within its boundaries. We come up with 1,000 reasons why our participation is worthless, justifying why we choose to not vote, we choose not to accept formal education, we choose to never work for others again but yet never actually come up with an alternative form of mastery. Instead, we simply reject our master. The issue is we are still very much reliant on that master, regardless that our belief forces us to take in that we do not want to be bound to a cage.

Since we have no way out, we stay attached to its attributes. I used the hamster as an example because such thinking is very two-dimensional in nature, a way of thinking of those who have yet to master circumstance. If the hamster rejects the idea that it's in a cage (bound to a master gatekeeper), the hamster cannot simply get out and leave. It is still bound to the cage, even if it realizes the cage is preventing it from becoming all it can be. In addition, the hamster will continue to give up aspirations of escaping the cage once its survival is re-established by being fed and given water. We feel the same when we lose a job we were given. Yet, when a new job is obtained, we simply conform to our established behavior without considering that the same behavior will most likely lead to the same outcome. This issue is because instead of seeking growth, **man is seeking survival in a world or society it doesn't understand, without trying to understand it.**

Societal traps are not really traps; they are boundaries of control created by other four-dimensional thinkers to ensure two-dimensional thinkers have a baseline of direction to follow. While they may seem deceiving in the way they are presented, they are actually not. An individual simply has to understand how to think in a four-dimensional matter in order to overcome them. They are not deceiving but those who have learned how to leverage them are. In other words:

You do not distrust the formal education system; you distrust the school that sold you on the potential results of following through with a degree.

You do not distrust or hate the idea of having faith or someone's religion; you distrust the people and churches who leverage faith in order to gain profits.

You do not hate the idea of government; you hate those who lie only to get into office.

We spoke earlier of the definitions that bound us to understanding the world around us, and this case is no different. By understanding the overall pictures and seeing how others create boundaries of control within such mechanisms, then we understand how the systems work. While we disagree entirely with most of them, our role isn't to revolt around them but rather to master them for an opportunity to eventually change them.

Think of life as playing a simple ten-stage video game with society being stage three. You cannot progress to stage four and eventually finish the game if you don't play the game in order, overcoming each stage as they are presented. We do not choose the order in which a video game is presented, so we must learn to master each stage. The same happens in life. While we do not choose the circumstance we are born into, the parents we are given, or the social status of acceptance. We choose how we move forward in life and we choose what we make of it even if we disagree.

The whole idea here is to no longer look at society as a giant trap or cage, but rather as a stage of life that must be overcome. This perspective must be accepted in order to shift our minds from a state of dependency on a master to dependency on ourselves for mastery.

Politics: Influence Over Wisdom or Deceit

Dating back to the Persian Empire, fourth-dimensional beings have attempted to change man's path in hopes that civilization would become more aligned to a path of wisdom. Known today as gods, biblical figures, and other mystical beings, most of the people we idolize today have influenced man's path for quite some time. The question remains, if they were gods and if they could change the world, then why did they need to reach our political figures in hopes of creating change through their leadership rather than forcing change on mankind? This has even become to date the argument as to the validation of "God's existence" and it can be summed up by this question:

"If those we call gods and worship have the power that we have expected of them, then why are they allowing suffering in the world?"

In order to be able to answer this, we have to look at our very own dimensional opportunity going back to the idea of "Are we gods to a snail?"

Earlier, we covered the vast differences in speeds between the snail and the human, giving the human a god-like figure over the snail since its entire lifetime lies within a one-dimensional realm and ours in a three-dimensional space.

So, can we actually end the suffering for all snails, and, if so, why do we not? Is it that we do not care? Is it that one snail isn't going to alter the ecosystem enough for us to give it our undivided attention?

Perhaps it is that we cannot understand the snail enough to decipher its state of being. In other words, we have absolutely no idea if a snail is happy, sad, or suffering. In many cases, as a society cares for the well-being of the ecosystem we live in and even the snail's ability to survive, we cannot help snails individually. This disconnect from the state of being of another dimensional being is perhaps the same for us human, in the context to those we refer to as gods. Perhaps it isn't in the lack of care or compassion that they ignore our suffering and us, but rather, through this suffering, we can choose how to experience life.

As a result, we take on an approach to protect our ecosystem, rather than our personal well-being. We do find more about ourselves in times of hardship than we do in times of comfort and happiness, as often wisdom is required to overcome hardship. To evolve past a state of suffering, often wisdom is no longer sought after when we have given ourselves to masters and traded our future evolution for comfort.

It is only when the comfort is stripped away that we are reminded of our lack of wisdom. This is no different than the hamster example, with its inability to realize it is a prisoner in a cage because the hamster is provided its basic needs of survival and therefore accepts the cage as its home, rather than a prison. Once its food is removed, it is then reminded of the reality of its lack of capacity to be free and to seek its own solution. It is only then that the hamster has the opportunity to gain wisdom to evolve by seeing the truth.

This scenario is no different than those of us with jobs who believe our work matters and accept our employers, despite their attempts at preventing our evolution. Only when fired or abandoned by such people do we realize that our survival was never dependent on them, but rather made easy by them. So, we accepted our prison because our survival depended on it—or so we thought—and even believed such prison to be beautiful at times.

Gods or not, those who have come in hopes of aligning civilization have come to those we elect as our masters. They do not come to those who need them the most. In that gesture alone lies many of the answers we perhaps seek of those we call gods themselves.

Think about the majority of the times we have seen an intervention, from the freeing of the Persian Empire's slave population (Zarathustra) to fixing the poverty inequality (Jesus) that existed during the era of the Roman Empire. Those we call "gods" had never come to fix man's suffering but rather to ensure humanity's trajectory. It is perhaps in this very simple gesture that we can understand that their role has never been to save humanity or even help it. Their role was to ensure nothing came in between man and his ability to awaken by protecting the ecosystem itself.

If the fourth dimension is time, then the fifth dimension becomes parallels of time, possibilities of timelines and directions that time in itself can take like a multiverse. As three-dimensional beings, we can acknowledge a fourth dimension but not actually hold any relevant physical impact on it. The same logic should technically apply to those four-dimensional beings who can see the impacts of time and any of its possible directions but can only impact their own current timelines. Having a view of how time is shifting the future and having full access to time would enable you to alter the future of those who have yet to experience it as they are travelling through time at a much slower rate. That said, the goal of such a mission would be to ensure the advancement of a civilization, rather than one single person.

This explains why so many prayers go unanswered. In themselves, prayers are often a result of a need for freedom from masters, and not a quest for wisdom.

Most people pray for health when they are sick, for money when they are poor, and for love when they are alone. Man often doesn't rely on God when not in a time of need. Instead, he gives in to masters on an ongoing basis, giving up aspirations of wisdom only to be given a state of comfort by his masters.

The reason prayer doesn't work is because it's an act of alchemy (more on this later) based on deceit, not on wisdom. When man is abandoned by his masters, he turns to find yet another master that will fill his needs. Why does man turn to his societal leaders for guidance and only turn to other masters in churches when all others have failed them, and finally to God when even the church fails them? In this quest for answers, man gives in to worship rather than wisdom. Through this state of deceit, he finds himself abandoned by all those he worshiped.

We must understand that evolution is not about falling victim to obedience and worship. We must acknowledge that societal and religious leaders are not there to help us reach God, or even a higher state of being, but rather to give us an outlet to get rid of our suffering. It is when we accept that we want others to free us from suffering that we accept their boundaries of control. We then give up our aspirations for reaching higher levels of wisdom that would have given us the ability to remove ourselves from that very same state of suffering once and for all. The journey to evolution in itself is difficult and requires work. As a result, it is forgotten by the masses in exchange for the temporary relief from suffering.

While gods may or may not exist and their existence may be our very own selves in a different dimension, the reality of society is that its existence is a mechanism for growth for all three-dimensional beings, regardless of their acceptance or rejection. A collective of laws and powers is given by the masses to the few, in an attempt to create order and common advancement for all. Since the majority of beings seek comfort over wisdom, they will often elect leaders who promise them a higher state of comfort over wisdom. Ones who seeks deceit, will often find others who deceive them, while those who seek wisdom will often find others who challenge them.

Anyone who understands politics and society knows that the common interest of the masses is the farthest goal for those in power. We fail to realize the importance of politics in our day-to-day lives, as they are very much a part of the daily routines we must learn to abide by.

Regardless of where you come from, the money you have accumulated, or the level of awareness you possess, you will forever be in a state of collective expectations. You must understand that existing in a three-dimensional state requires your compliance to the rules set forth by those in power.

Compliance isn't the same as obedience; the majority of the population falls in a state of obedience, the Higher Man falls in a state of compliance. He doesn't rely on masters to craft his aspiration but rather understanding that theological evolution isn't established by the defiance of politics, but rather its mastery. Those who reject the basic principles of politics will spend their lifetime in a state of war, internally and externally, which prevents their own internal growth. **Politics, no matter how loved or hated, is an internal control system created in hopes of allowing order and consistency in the world through dialogue.** It is no different than those who pray to God only when in need. Most people rely on politics and the State only when it is convenient and to their advantage, often disagreeing with a direction chosen unless of course it benefits them.

This is the exact issue with the majority of society as a whole, we have gotten to a state where we no longer care about the common evolution of our civilization but rather choose to make political arguments about the boundaries of false comfort and security created. As a result, we elect officials from a state of deceit who end up deceiving us. It is in the intention of our action that the same intent is reciprocated.

While not all men are crafted to be politicians, all men should be aware of the politics they are required to play and progress through society. Politics are the influence beings have on one another; that influence can sway an entire civilization into its own deceit and collapse. It is a system built on the foundation that we must learn to care for the collective consciousness as much as we care for ourselves. We must learn through politics that there is more at stake than our own comfort, but rather the basis for advancement for those of us who cannot advance. We can fix this with a simple act of influence and more importantly participation.

Participation: An Opportunity to Free Others

Participating in politics doesn't require running for office or becoming an elected official. It is more aligned with one's view of society and its role in the grand scheme of evolution. As explained in *Third Circle Theory*, man's awareness and capacity for evolution comes from his ability to overcome circumstance in the first stage of life, where he is led by his fears. He is challenged again in the Second Circle by having to master the mechanisms of society, not by circumventing it but by learning to master it. Everything from the mastery of wealth, societal reputation, and the opportunity for deceit is challenged in this Second Circle.

When man chooses wisdom over deceit and learns the boundaries of control that prevent others who have never yet committed to mastery and excellence, he then finds himself with an opportunity to advance to the Third Circle. This is a place where man can give birth to a new version of himself, one bound by mastery of creativity, one that enables others living in the first and Second Circle to unite around him in his creation. It is in this creation that man realizes with clarity the boundaries that other masters have created for the control of the masses. It is in this stage that man can choose to become a master or help others reach a higher level of mastery to free them. It is in this moment that one realizes the importance of participation in the realm of society as a means to progressing onward.

Participation in society comes from the ability to fit in as personalities in society are formed and shaped, based on the delusions of our internal EGO. One cannot progress to shed their EGO without facing it and realizing what the EGO is protecting them from. Those who ignore such participation are essentially attempting to skip a very important part of their own journey, the part that allows them to define the difference between their personality and their EGO. **Man must perceive the difference between the EGO, which allows them to survive, and the SELF that allows them to transition.** They gain the ability to shed the EGO from the mastery of it, not the rejection or avoidance of what the EGO stands for.

Compare man's evolutionary journey of societal mastery to man's journey in search of purpose. Man is attempting to first fit in and to learn how to use and manipulate his skills and talents. He is given purpose by others until he is ready to commit to his very own. The practice is essential or it is possible that when man faces his chosen purpose, he may not be in a state of awareness that enables him the confidence and talent to pursue it (often referred to as "not being ready to seize the opportunity"). Participating in society gives us the opportunity to not only understand but also practice using our EGO and allowing our SELF to gain confidence while doing so.

Confidence: A Tool to Break Free From Our Masters

Often misunderstood for arrogance by those who lack the most of it, confidence is one of the masterful tools that we, as humans, get to generate within the boundaries of control in our early phases of life. Gaining confidence is the result of a controlled practice in a limited environment. One of the reasons many people do not develop confidence is their inability to leverage those same control mechanisms because they deny that such mechanisms exist.

Control mechanisms are meant to limit your motion and thought to the confines of those boundaries, forcing you to focus in order to seek mastery. Believe it or not, such mechanisms are important to the baseline of many humans who lose focus very fast these days because of an overload of input (more on this later).

Next, let's look at how the boundaries of control can be used to our advantage to enable progressive confidence to go from a state of non-existence to a state of mastery.

If someone were to attempt to make new friends or get a date at a bar, most people would be bar-hopping over and over, hoping for more luck or a better environment to fuel their confidence. One of the mistakes here is that environment will not change the outcome or the person's confidence, but rather become a game of luck, which is more like gambling than growing. However, if you visited the same bar every single night and sat in the exact same chair every day, you would be collecting data on an ongoing basis, furthering your chances of meeting those you seek.

You could observe who comes in, what they are drinking, the behaviors of those who are having success at meeting people, and with every failure, you would add yet another data point for what *not* to do. This means that every attempt is one more step towards succeeding because the only variable changing each and every time is you. Therefore, you can evolve into the person who manipulates your environment in order to get what you want, rather than expects your environment to help you attain what you want.

Removing yourself from one environment and planting yourself in another after having had success demonstrates the ability to duplicate the process time and time again with even fewer attempts. This strength gives you an opportunity to gain confidence in this one ability, being that you are the one who figured out the "how to" and not just the essence of being in the right place at the right time.

We can judge the same equation in business as well. When we start a business focused in one industry and it does not work, we can choose to move on or we can choose to attempt to figure it out. Once more, we pick a new environment to master rather than master ourselves into figuring out our existing choice of environment.

When we master the business by succeeding, we once more figure out the formula required, thus gaining the confidence to feel we can duplicate it again. The more confidence, the bigger the undertaking, which is why it is often necessary to remember that confidence is progressive, just as much as success in any context is. Undertaking smaller goals will lead to more confidence to undertake larger ones.

This confidence concept is often misunderstood by those who live in such similar boundaries and yet are still relying on their environment to help them gain confidence. When exposed to others who have already figured out the formula to growth and progress, some will tend to think that the confidence exhibited by one to help others is arrogance.

For confidence to foster in any human being, we must be able to leverage those boundaries of control to enable our focus to remain on one task at a time. The reasons these boundaries even exist in our lives is to enable us to master them faster, as boundaries at a young age are much smaller than the boxes we create as adults in our lives. We must first learn to function in a two-dimensional environment so that enough mastery exists by the time we go to a four-dimensional one. At that point, boundaries are constantly created and destroyed internally, instead of being forced on our thoughts. **The more confidence we accumulate, the easier it becomes to make decisive choices in life** that we choose to stand behind.

Belief: An Absolute Boundary Based on Yesterday's Choice

The most powerful opportunity man has is to always keep an open mind to information he is presented, not to understand opinions but rather to see possibilities. When we think of truth, we tend to think of the word "belief". Our belief fuels our truth. That truth we accept leads us to creating our original boundary of control. While we can expand such boundaries with new experiences over time, we typically don't venture too far from the original belief that set us there. One can grow up in a religious family, bound by the rules and standards established by any such religion. While over time one can be flexible on how often he practices such faith or how committed he remains to it, in the end, he still ends up setting his reality based on those same boundaries; he will not completely stop living his life through that same set of rules.

The same can be established of many other things, like our view of government, politics, education, and more. If one's belief is set on the idea that formal education is the primary way one reaches success, then that truth becomes a boundary of control, meaning that it now becomes "the way" one can find success. The more observations are set on that truth over time, based on environment—meaning the more we are exposed to this being a reality in our world—the more concrete the truth becomes and the more established this boundary of control becomes. The result changes from "the way" to "the *only* way" one becomes successful. The belief fuels the accepted truth, and often is as a result of not seeing past your own environment.

This is an easy conversation to have, as it pertains to basic, small, harmless elements like education or politics. It can be much deeper than that when coupled with the concept of boundaries as they pertain to values and ethics. We can go to a much deeper state of thought, where we question things like murder or terrorism.

On the surface, these acts would seem to be condemned by reasonable men, regardless of their religious beliefs. One can argue that, regardless of their belief, there is no justifiable choice to take a life that wasn't his to take. One can also debate that God is the one to make such a decision, but then again, another could present the opinion that this act was God's plan for those people to be there at that time and place. They could assert that there is no God and that the act was of pure randomness. All can be saddened by the situation and can argue their belief and truth to be the boundary they set forth on how they accept the act that occurred. The act, while very tragic, is defined differently in the minds of the three individuals who all maintain different boundaries of control.

We can also go even further as it pertains to the boundaries of control by looking at the absolute truth as it relates to choice. Most of us can reasonably state that murdering another is a bad choice, and most could argue that if put in such situation, we would not make such a choice. However, even choice in itself holds a ripple effect based on the boundaries of control we set. When we live under any such boundaries, we have hard limitations that differentiate a good versus a bad choice, often because boundaries of control are set to revolve around ourselves. We question choice based on our perspective of control, failing to acknowledge that we are even under such a control mechanism. Let's look at the ripple effects and structures of what seems to be a somewhat obvious choice. Believe me when I say, this section may need your review multiple times to truly be understood without an emotional reaction.

We reject the act of terrorism and often blame extremists for such violent and cowardly acts. It's very easy to end the conversation there because of our similar alignments in thoughts about murder. But what if the choice we think each of these people has to make is very different when analyzed from a different boundary of control? As mentioned earlier, truth is perspective.

A man walks into a building and detonates a vest packed with explosives, killing 20 people. We blame him for the action, and we blame the group that enabled him to perform the act. This basic, two-dimensional thought does not take in effect our four-dimensional opportunity to understand the time basis of the choice. We judge the choice based on the action from point A to Point B.

However, we have the capacity to see farther than that. We have the ability to analyze the timeline of choice that would hold more weight on the way the choice was made. Look at that same person living at the age of 10 in his village, surrounded by an army fighting a war he wants no part of. His country is in desperate need of a political win, which is the assassination of one person in that village who is deemed a serious threat. The military calls an airstrike to level off the majority of that one village to kill that one individual. That strike delivers the collateral damage and deaths of 100 innocent people, including the entire family of that child. He alone survives.

At age 10, he roams an empty field in search of the truth he was taught to believe and finds nothing but the end of the life he knew. In that same field, a man with a helping hand promises shelter, education, food, and an opportunity to understand what just happened. This man doesn't fight wars with drones, fighter jets, or high-end weaponry. He fights it with conviction and belief. Here is a man willing to foster, influence, and convince a young man's mind for over 20 years about the best and most powerful way to live life. He fosters a new boundary of control for the boy—a new "truth". Isolated from the ability to gain a different perspective over that timeframe, the boy grows into a man who sets a new boundary. He accepts that his attack that day is the choice to help restore the balance. He does not view it as an act of terror, but rather one of justice.

Now, you tell me if he made the right choice or not.

What you must understand is that choice is based on your absolute truth, your boundary of control. If you are not consciously aware of that boundary and its existence, then you cannot consciously make a choice that reflects its possible ripple effect.

When you limit your mind's default setting from looking at the world from a two-dimensional space of action and reaction, you gain the opportunity to understand the timeline of how things occur. You also expand your boundary of truth from that of an animal that only understands what's in it for him to a subjective reality. This reality is not bound by the simplicity of saying "life is about making the right choices", but of understanding that choice in its nature is neutral, no matter how much you want to go back and justify it by its simple cause and effect.

We want to believe our boundary of control is the one the majority should follow. We also know there is not one way to get from point A to Point B, and there isn't a correct or incorrect way to get there. We recognize that while some paths may have seemed more effective at times than others, their effectiveness was based on their timeline as much as the way they were undertaken. By giving yourself an absolute truth to believe and to guide your direction and decision, you limit yourself to two-dimensional thinking and the worship of the master who has created such a conforming boundary for you to operate within. That boundary was never meant for you to stay in, but rather for you to learn how to master the components within before expanding and growing out of. We however have found comfort in the ideas of boundaries and control mechanisms that give us a sense of security and predictability.

For example, the majority of us no longer seek to buy weapons to protect ourselves but rather rely on the law and police to do so. We no longer strive for continuous learning but rather depend on the formal education system to prepare us for the work it wants us to do.

Either of these two examples are basic concepts yet continue to plague our world as we all establish various absolute truths to follow. As a result, the examples divide one from the other by being more focused on tribal acceptance and belonging, than to unify each other into one dimension. One place where we all accept that the only absolute truth is that the time our personalities have to develop is limited. Each opportunity leads to our acceptance that the next is defined by the choices we made in time, not in the right or wrong we perceived to have lived by.

Self-Awareness: The Birth of Personality

In *Third Circle Theory*, I introduced you to the evolution of the mind from the state of conformity to the state of self-awareness and the power of leveraging observations to help facilitate that journey. While I covered the power of discovery, I didn't touch on the evolution of the psyche through the same transformation.

For those of you who may not be familiar with my work, the concept is simply the understanding that each human being has to overcome himself three times in order to evolve. The first evolution signifies the mastery of Circumstance, the second is the mastery of Society and the third, the mastery of Oneself. While most would assume that mastery of life is achieved once you enter the Third Circle of the journey, it is quite the opposite, the beginning of the opportunity of mastery then begins. The connection of the journey is the ability to make sense of the boundary that connects body and psyche. While on the surface it may seem like a road map to awareness, it is a road map to defining the SELF, giving a sense of self-awareness instead.

Most people seem to confuse awareness with self-awareness. Definitions in society are rather blurred, based on their constant usage in the wrong format. We even confuse words like "business" and "entrepreneurship" or concepts like "church" and "faith". Awareness is one's ability to pay attention and understand their environment. This has been made much easier today, thanks to more cameras, more information, and more sharing of what's happening in the world, allowing us to be more conscious of what is happening around us. We can receive and decipher more information at once than ever before. Self-awareness, on the other hand, is the ability to understand the impact of one's being on the environment they occupy. In other words, you are conscious of who you are, therefore understanding how others perceive you. You realize that the SELF is the accepted reality of the image others have of you, and therefore you and ONLY you hold the power to change the SELF as you want. You can consciously change and impact your environment and the perspective of those around you. While we live in a world with a significant increase in awareness, we also live in a world where more and more people struggle to find themselves because they are incapable of controlling their input-output. The majority of people are aware of what's happening but don't know how or what to do to impact their environment. This is called "input overload".

The mind is set to receive information, process it, and then choose a pattern of action. This basic concept is what I refer to as the "input–output concept". Information goes in, action comes out. The issue is that for most people, the information goes in, and no action comes out. This is an issue of bridging the gap between awareness and self-awareness—the issue of finding function and success in society. When too much information goes in, the mind cannot analyze it fast enough and is still processing a way to channel it out. Before it can do so, even more information is received. This is what causes information paralysis and prevents someone from finding a focus point. The reason this is so common isn't because we are in an age of information but rather because we are in an age where practicing output has become very difficult. **We are in an age of instant gratification and expect the output to occur at the same pace or speed as the input, which is impossible.**

There are two basic components to help restore this balance in most.

Skills: Skills are the baseline for how output is created. If you have no skills to connect input to output, you receive input and do not know how to connect output. Think of having a great business idea that involves making a website. If you have coding skills, you can immediately take action and that need for an immediate output is met with the same velocity as the input. The ability to act quickly only occurs because you have relevant skills. This is the reason many people never find success in business. They pick ideas unrelated to their capacity or skills, and therefore give up quickly as no output is ever created fast enough to create a direction of action.

Learn to say "no": The baseline of focus comes from the ability to turn input into *selective* input, meaning the ability to seek out more information on the same topic rather than allow your environment to set you up for even more unrelated input. If you get excited about a business idea that is about starting a website, you need to focus your mind on selecting more information on this topic only and learning to say "no" to other information, no matter how interesting it appears to be. It's committing to one idea, rather than keeping your options open. The more you say "no" to unrelated information, the more focused your input approach becomes, while also becoming more controlled.

The basic input-output concept is one of the critical steps necessary to become more self-aware. The more output is created, the more SELF is discovered. Output creates a data point. Think of data points as practice points. The more you practice something, the more you understand or generate data. With a video game, for example, the more you play the game, the more you can anticipate the moves of the other players or the computer playing against you. These data points enable you to anticipate and plan ahead.

It's no different than our discussion of dimensional points. The only difference between an animal and a human is the conscious ability to understand time, which gives us the ability to predict and plan our occupation of space at a certain point in time. The same power must be used when collecting data points. The more we practice something, the more conscious we become of every possible outcome, and the more focused we become on understanding how to create the outcome we want, not repeating the same failed data points.

This journey of practicing output gives us a significant amount of data points that lead us to gaining more self-awareness. The issue for most is the fear of failure that underscores the collection of such data points. This fear is coupled with the inability to understand that you must collect these data points and become numb to the idea of failure. Without failure, there can be no data points so the failure isn't an option, but rather part of the process.

Input leads to data to create more favorable outputs. The output creates an image of the SELF. This process, while simple in theory, requires a massive level of self-understanding and is filled with emotional rejection, which you must learn to look past. Self-awareness is a journey that is launched with your continuous ability to define your intention and words, align your perspective to the lack of an absolute truth and control your focus through balancing your input and output. While most think that becoming self-aware is the destination, they miss the idea that the birth of the bridge between the Last Man and the Superman (man's ultimate and final form which we will discuss later) only becomes visible to those who start seeing the world through a self-aware lens.

Philosophy: A Map to Becoming Conscious

Man seeks direction, guidance and a path to freedom, but often forgets that the freedom he seeks is a new boundary of control—one built on someone else's baseline of control.

We seek steps to freedom through government, only to be given safety in exchange for obedience.

We seek the path to financial freedom through education, only to be given a salary for our compliance.

We seek leadership to guide our growth in Corporate America only to be left obeying yet a new directive.

We seek guidance on how to live through those who preach faith only to be given yet another master to obey.

Man no longer is given an opportunity to transcend himself, but instead has been given a path to safety, obedience, and compliance. He has been taught to not live dangerously, not take chances, not venture outside of those boundaries of control that jeopardize and risk his safety. **To be brave, to be exemplary, to be fearless is no longer an expectation of the many, but rather an achievement of the few.**

In order for man to break free of this curse of a quest for safety rather than aspiration, man must be willing to accept that the path to finding one's self is not given or taught by yet another master but rather through mastery of one's self.

One such tool we have to be able to welcome mastery in our life is to seek guidance through philosophy, to analyze and understand the boundaries created by those masters. We learn to break free of the masters by giving up this idea of an absolute truth. Abandon the idea that our life is defined by a boundary of right and wrong. Accept that our personality is and always has been shaped by our past environment. It can now be shaped by our choices rather than our circumstances, giving up this need for masters in our lives all together and instead becoming masters of our lives through mastery.

Philosophy doesn't teach us what to do but rather shows us how others have done, enabling us to understand from a broader perspective the interaction between those who gave in to control and those who controlled others. Ask not from masters how to get to a destination but rather from philosophy how to overcome the road ahead.

Excellence: A Bridge to Aspiration

Aspiration is mankind's secret weapon, the understanding that we are meant to be more than we understand. To aspire isn't to dream, but rather to transcend. Mankind in its last centuries has slowly started to forget what it's like to aspire and, as a result, has given in to the boundaries of control it has been given in order to secure its own safety and comfort. While many have chosen this path, we are not all bound to suffer the same fate and can change the directions of our lives, even if they are headed to the same outcome. Aspiration, in its more fundamental form, is to understand and accept that man can be more than what he is today. If you have so far understood the path of the dimensional evolution we all undertake, then perhaps you are now also looking for the best way to get there.

One of the most effective ways we can continue to guarantee our evolution from a state of control to a state of free will is to commit to the basic idea of excellence.

Excellence as a bridge to aspiration.

Excellence is the hidden bridge that gives birth to meaning and purpose. In *Third Circle Theory*, I break down the idea that purpose—although many want to believe is divine in nature—is a human being's ability to accept his role in the space he occupies at any given time. While purpose is assigned to us in the earlier stages of our lives, it becomes a choice later for those of us who understand that **the most powerful path we undertake in life is the one we choose rather than the one we are given.** A commonly accepted perception holds that, at some point in time and space, a divine intervention will showcase itself to us. Instead, we should focus on our ability to identify the opportunity rather than wait for random act. This in itself is the essence of this entire book. The concept that choice, including how we perceive things, is what leads us to the transcendence of our vessel and the vessel's return to the source.

One of the most powerful ways we can ensure that our path for growth and evolution is maintained is to commit to excellence. We achieve this through purpose, by ensuring that—regardless of whether we are given a purpose or choose one in space—we accept its relevant time connection and accomplish it with the highest level of excellence. While many people today will argue that the early stages of their lives are not what they want for themselves (often seen in people with jobs, rather than careers), they will simply not perform their best. They never really allow themselves to accept their position in time and space at that moment.

They allow time to flow forward as they are bound to its arrow but make no use of the space they occupy. They rely on their hopes that they will occupy a more relevant one at some point later. While many of us are most likely not going to end our paths in the same place we have started, we can agree that occupying space while ignoring the fact that time moves forward is the same as not being conscious that time exists, once again no different than an animal that has no concept of time.

Excellence in itself is the attempted evolution and mastery of each control mechanism we encounter during our journey. By committing to the mastery of such control mechanisms, we can graduate past them faster. We also allow our scope of controls to become much larger, until we reach a state where we are faced with the creation of our own control mechanism. At this point, we no longer rely on the others created for us to obey masters. The more we excel in all aspects of our lives, the more deeply we get to reinforce our confidence and the farther we are able to see. The ability to see farther in our own lives and the ecosystems of control around us enables us to adopt the basis for what we refer to as "vision". As excellence gives birth to vision, vision enables man to aspire because of his belief of what *can be*, not of *what is*. This brings us to the beginning of the journey of what a Higher Man's role truly is.

One who aspires to bring a vision to life gives life meaning and it is in the progress towards meaning where man holds the ultimate key to his own happiness, consciousness, and choice.

PART II: The Creator

Aspiration: The Never-Ending Quest for Wisdom

“Slavery should not be allowed, as for an enslaved body cannot give birth to a free mind.” —Zarathustra

When man finds himself aware of the masters who have kept him mentally enslaved, he comes to terms with the idea that freedom comes in three basic steps: The freeing of the mind, the escape from society, and the birth of consciousness. These three steps are led forward by one’s ability to tap into excellence and creativity. In this next section, we will explore the definitions that enable man to find a path to mastery, and how mastery through entrepreneurship can become the tool necessary to evolve from an enslaved body to a free mind.

Meaning: Journey to Mastery

The purpose of existence has always been a question mark amongst all men. Why do we exist? What is our given purpose? What does God have in store for me?

While most pose the question, few attempt to answer it. The idea of purpose is hardly as complicated as some believe. Those who forfeit their lives to masters will patiently wait for a sign, an indication that their chosen path is the correct one. Those committed to mastery and an understanding of their time-based experiences will look at it quite differently.

Perhaps purpose was never about an alignment to one's journey, but rather an alignment to one's state of mind and the power of creating purposeful experiences for others and us.

There are two types of purposes in life: One that is accepted and one that is chosen. While both are equally important, the accepted states of purpose throughout your life enable you to reach a mental state of choice that eventually allows you to transition to a chosen purpose.

Purpose, as defined in the *Third Circle Theo*ry, is defined as a man's acceptance of his role in a specific given time and space continuum. While you may not always have chosen your purpose, you have accepted to assume the role. For example, you may not choose to be someone's son or daughter, but you are born into that role. You may not have an array of choices when it comes to certain jobs you accept in your lifetime, but you have nonetheless accepted the role. You still hold the choice to honor such a role or not, but that choice is what will define your progress towards giving your life meaning. **It isn't in the choice itself, but rather in the acceptance of it that man moves closer to mastery.**

Humans who are bound by masters struggle to understand this basic concept that purpose isn't given to a person, but rather to a state of acceptance. It is simply the idea that one who is bound by a master will often wait for such master to assign them a purpose. Conversely, those pursuing mastery will undertake various purposes with the intention of mastering character and to establish a personal opportunity to choose a desired purpose, rather than wait for the next one to be given to them.

To find one's purpose isn't truly life's meaning. It is a tool one can use to establish a sense of higher aspiration, to be given the belief and power to break free of existing limitations.

When man is charged with purpose, he has an opportunity to allow aspiration to lead his path from a world bound by masters to a world dominated by mastery.

It is the greatest force in the universe and the shaping guide to turning hard limitations into flexible opportunities.

When a man of purpose accepts his chosen purpose, he allows aspiration to become the leading force to giving meaning to his life. He therefore measures progress towards such purpose as the baseline for happiness, rather than focusing on activities that lead to the passage of time. He no longer attempts to give his life meaning through the boundary of time, but rather meaning through immortality of his reputation.

Reputation: Man's Imprint on Time

Reputation—often misunderstood from the EGO standpoint as our standing amongst our other humans—is the imprint of our legacy beyond the existence of our vessel. While most think of legacy as leaving a business behind, we must think of reputation from the standpoint of leaving a piece of our personality behind. We do so by understanding that businesses of any sort are an extension of our personalities. Unfortunately, even they can forever be altered by future personalities coming in past our existence and taking away such imprint forever. One such solution to the mortality of our businesses is to understand that **creativity is the essence of the imprint, not business.**

We can identify some of today's most honored and remembered psyches based on their creative contributions to the world. Everyone from Disney to Van Gogh have been remembered not for their business models but rather their art, and what it meant to those who experienced it.

In their time, their art wasn't appreciated by the masses for its validity of society, but its ability to allow others a glimpse into their own aspirations.

The imprint of their reputation remains today a beacon of aspiration for Higher Humans today who not only see the creative efforts of others but can also gain a perspective of time through their work. This is exhibited from the evolution of art showing glorious and powerful beings with freedom and light to today's darker art showing oppression, boundary and frustration. The art is still a creative effort and contributes to the reputation of many on all parts. It is also a timeline, an imprint that tells a story of evolution or lack thereof.

Each aspect of auto manufacturing tells a similar story. Take Ferrari, for example. With each model that Ferrari releases, its timeline continues the story. Each car reflects a racing pedigree, continuing to the more recent focus on consumerism and the ability to sell more cars than ever before. History is being rewritten everyday by corporations that are changing the direction of those very same companies that were initially created as someone's art. It is, however, the impact their art has had that will forever become the imprint of their reputation.

More importantly, such creativity lived beyond their reputations. They gave hope to other Higher Humans. These Higher Humans found it harder and harder to connect to the rest of the diminishing population, those who welcomed the Herd. They remained connected more to their creative genius within. As humanity folded, man found less and less aspiration, and as a result found a way to survive the decline in civilization through a state of Roush.

Roush: The Capacity to Identify Aspiration

Someone once asked me why I was materialistic. I answered that I do not consider myself materialistic at all. I have a need for beauty in my life, and such beauty cannot be found in creations made for the Herd but rather through the imprint of someone's reputation.

The more dimensional awareness man has, the more he disconnects from others. In the quest for unity, man can only unite with those on the same vibration level. For that reason, Higher Humans struggle to connect as the majority of humanity lived as part of the Herd, satisfied by the idea of being the Last Man. While connectivity to each other gets more and more scarce as you evolve, the overall connection to humanity also gets weaker as a whole. As a result, man hides his disconnect and state of loneliness by allowing himself to substitute connection for Roush.

Roush is a state of aspiration that comes from the art of beauty. When man knows himself best, he finds himself travelling through a journey filled with darkness and light. This journey, while intense and powerful for the psyche, must be survived from a vessel standpoint, the origin of this state. Think of it as finding a beautiful rose in the middle of a hurricane. While embarking on a journey of self-discovery, man longs for beauty as a reminder of the light in his life. The reaction of internal peace, which comes from this beauty, is what we describe as the "state of Roush".

In my own theological evolution, I have consistently surrounded myself with beautiful things—from incredibly good-looking exotic cars to watches, art and people. This aesthetic need for beauty is what allowed me to survive the depth of the darkness that formed within me as a I evolved. Even today, I find it difficult to survive in environments that aren't aesthetically pleasing. From my office to my home, order and design hold the highest relevance.

While those who have not travelled through my path may describe my intention as materialism, those who have travelled to my awareness level recognize the beauty I surround myself with as a means to triggering more aspiration. The ability to control the trigger is what enables the capacity for self-growth. Even in times of financial stress, I exposed myself to beauty, even if ownership was not possible, based on my lack of capacity. I allowed myself to experience everything from visiting dealerships to visiting seven-figure homes and touching and feeling beauty that wasn't then aligned to my actual lifestyle.

The difference isn't in the design, but rather the *meaning* of the reputation that is seen from another lens as you evolve towards accepting your role as a Higher Human. I do not find beauty in status or fame; I find beauty in the art form of creation. When Honda makes a car, it does so in hopes of gaining market share and providing transportation. When Lamborghini makes a car, it does so to evoke a feeling and it is the art of creating a feeling that I can identify someone else's reputation and more importantly aspiration.

I surround myself with beauty so that I may be reminded of the creativity of others who have travelled a similar path, for they have created art through their aspiration that does not just appeal to me, but rather gives me a sense of peace.

While it is a state of Roush that man uses to overcome his darkness and steer clear of its pull, it is his quest for the mastery of himself that allows him to continue to push for his aspiration, breaking free of any form of masters. Man is best when he is creative than when he is bound, which is why before he can fully master himself, he must first master his aspiration through his ability to create.

Imagination: The Ability to Draw Our Own Boxes

As man becomes inspired, he pushes for the pursuit of excellence in all he does but when man finds aspiration, he pushes for the pursuit of creation. Man's boundary of control comes from a state of awareness that is built of comfort and fear, and while man gives up his need for mastery to a master, he also imprisons his mind through this process, seeking guidance and direction always from the same master.

Regardless that it is God, church, Corporate America or an authoritative figure, man always finds himself in state of limbo where progress doesn't take place towards his meaning in order to give birth to purpose. This disconnect is the by-product of waiting for a master to assign a destination. However, the master cannot do so because the idea of a destination outside of the box would mean shattering the box of control and providing true freedom.

This is partially why people find themselves discontent with working a career for others for ten or more years, only to realize that they are stuck. When you start a new career, you find yourself in a situation where there is enough immediate growth that the illusion of your box expanding keeps you going forward. Still, at some point, you reach a state where the growth no longer arrives with the same speed. In its place comes these longer periods of waiting where your excellence is required to keep your job and yet is never met by your imagination because progress slows down.

This breakdown in process reminds man that perhaps he never had a destination to begin with, and that his box of control never expanded as he once thought it did. Instead, man was allowed to roam free in a larger box that he could not aspire to see. When man realizes that he is trapped in a box that strips him of his imagination, he realizes that he no longer has a destination and starts losing his aspiration.

Such loss leads to more acceptance of complacency and a state of settling that pushes him back to a state where he cannot overturn his circumstance (First Circle) rather than towards a state of self-mastery (Third Circle). It is only when man understands the power of creativity and its necessity to reinstate a new destination that he will seek to give his life meaning by separating his creativity from his boundary of control. He no longer seeks a new master but focuses on allowing mastery to define his limitation. It is in that moment that man connects the ability to create with a new destination in mind and accepts entrepreneurship into his life.

Entrepreneurship: Unity Around Creation

Most connect entrepreneurship to business, when in reality entrepreneurship is one's ability to bring creativity into the world and allow others to unify around their creation. In the end, entrepreneurship is the ability to connect one's self to aspiration and allow the creation to set forth the path to increasing your dimensional awareness and enabling your vessel to establish a reputation. This process is the ultimate lesson for man to take control of his creativity, excellence, and reputation and to give his life meaning, but more importantly, connect to the physical world.

It is through entrepreneurship that we discover what we are capable of.

It is through entrepreneurship that we shed our dependency on masters and rely on our own mastery to define our boundary of control, as **we have never been made to serve masters, but rather to imprint our mastery.**

While the Last Man laughs in ridicule of the Higher Man's attempt at earning his reputation through entrepreneurship, he laughs due to the fear that if the Higher Man succeeds, he will then be reminded of his very own boundary of control. It's no different than two inmates, both wanting to escape, but only one possessing the nerve to actually try. While both want to escape, one will wish the other one's failure so that he is not reminded that he should have had the courage to take on the journey.

Men who reject entrepreneurship are rejecting the idea of freedom from masters, for they have not acknowledged their power for creativity. They feel they are incapable of finding a direction without being given one. This is often due to their lack of commitment to a state of excellence that would have built their character to discover their internal creativity.

For entrepreneurship to become a path to the SELF, man must first master excellence and allow it to manifest itself past the creativity. He also needs to understand that, in this instance, he will learn the power of connecting the psyche to the vessel in a manner that will draw other vessels to him. In this way, he raises his dimensional awareness in the process. While, in society, entrepreneurship is a game of authority and power, it is internally a game of mastery. A game not played in the second dimension but rather one that allows man to evolve during this journey from a second to a third to a fourth dimension.

Most men look at life from a two-dimensional state, understanding that life has a beginning and ending. While there is truth to this, this two-dimensional approach is limiting for the mind. Even in a world where we seek to go from A to B, even point B is only a beginning, not the end. In thinking in just two dimensions, we limit our need to work past the ending and forget reputation. We focus on completion. While there is value in closing a chapter, there is greater value in how you lived through the chapter in excellence, rather than focused on completion. By projecting such a low dimensional awareness towards entrepreneurship, the goal of those who haven't yet mastered themselves is limited. They seek only a means to an end. Entrepreneurship, like life, isn't a two-dimensional game, but one built on four-dimensional progression. It is not driven by a means to an end but by the purpose one seeks to accept in this lifetime of establishing a reputation that lives past their physical existence.

Purpose: A Bridge to Mastery

With creativity coupled with excellence, man is able to give meaning to his life and establish a belief aligned to the reason for his existence. There may not be a way to verify or clarify if this purpose is one provided by a greater power, a pre-written contract, or divine in nature. However, we can understand that man connects more to who he is, based on his pursuit of purpose and the idea of being purposeful.

Man is willing to surrender himself when he is driven by a cause greater than his physical being. While man can be purposeful in all he does, it is only when man's purpose is actually chosen intentionally that he allows his being to surrender to the meaning he has given it. A conscious choice of such purpose is an acceptance of its meaning and impact. Through that surrender, man no longer seeks happiness through possessions, power, and control but through the progress he makes towards his destination.

When man chooses a destination, he forfeits the EGO and surrenders his true self to the idea that his time in his vessel isn't limited to the way he once believed and that creativity and excellence are the only drivers to his progress. He understands that the idea that his reputation will live past his physical existence, and that it allows him the opportunity to become a master, a master craftsman not of his own world but of a boundary of control that enables others to operate and work within.

As described in *Third Circle Theory*'s Second Circle analysis, when man is given the master of society, he is faced with a choice to remain there as a master or manipulator or to seek a greater outcome by entering the Third Circle. In this very same instance, when man is given the ability to create a boundary of control for others and take ownership of others, he is once more given the choice to manipulate and control or rather create a gateway of passage for others to grow. In other words, he chooses to become a master of control or to become a bridge of surrender for others who lack direction. One chooses to enslave others or help others transition, and it is within the intension that the choice is made.

If the choice is made to become a bridge, he will become the first to cross over it to a state of surrender. In that surrender, he must give up the limiting belief of time and its function as it pertains to progress. Instead, he welcomes the possibility that fourth-dimensional awareness and growth isn't just a possibility but rather inevitable and part of our evolutionary obligation. It is in that acceptance that his journey begins towards the Gate of Choice.

PART III: The Master

Theological Evolution: The Surrender of Physical Time

In this final part of *The Gate of Choice*, we will analyze the power of choosing as it pertains to our mastery, not our masters. We will understand the impact that such choices have as choice within a third-dimensional box has consequences only felt by the vessel. We will acknowledge that choices made with a fourth-dimensional state of mastery have consequences that could be felt through eternity as man was never put on earth to serve masters but rather learn to craft his own mastery. Then, he can give birth to the real SELF and its final forged personality.

Relativity: A Perception of Our Experiences

If my theory of time holds any relevance, then we understand that time takes place all at once. There is no real past, present, and future. Time has already taken its course in space at a faster pace. It is only our inability to break free of the boundaries of our vessel that forces us to experience time one space at a time, in one forward motion, which is why we are bound by the arrow of time as discussed earlier. Some scientists will argue that, if that were the case, then it renders free will useless. If an event has already taken its place, and then my free will changes it, the outcome wasn't the future to begin with. However, if it takes place as expected, then it renders my free will useless.

Both of these concepts have validity but what I propose is to not look at life from the lens of events occurring and their order in time and space, but the experiences and interpretations of them as they occur. An example can be seen at a wedding, where every guest already knows the outcome. They can predict the future with 99% certainty—the marriage—but the future doesn't become real until the experience is complete and the presiding clergy declares it. While we already know what is about to happen, it is the way we feel and experience the moment that determines its impact on our mind, personality, and awareness, and not the event itself.

If life were a simulation—like a video game—then we could say that all the levels are already preset, that levels one through ten are going to exist, no matter what your timeline is. Regardless of your strengths in levels one to three, you will still have to undergo levels four through ten. This process will not change. However, what will change is your ability to undertake these levels with more confidence, fear, or awareness as a result of the experiences you underwent in the first three levels, making the rest of the game more or less difficult for the remainder of its timeline.

The same can be assumed of life. How we deal with the earlier stages of life enables us to gain or lose competitive advantages as we move along the various levels we will face. While we always struggle with and worry about the future—what there is to come and what we may or may not experience—we already know our entire future. We know with certainty that we will die, deal with pain and sorrow, and even find happiness at various times. If we know these factually, then we can say with certainty that ***what* we experience isn't nearly as relevant as to *how* we experience it.** The how is what differentiates the personality we forge in this lifetime.

By understanding that time is relative not to your location in space but rather to your experience of it, we can drag time to last forever or cut our time short. It is up to us to understand that in this lifetime we have been given an opportunity to not just live through our time but rather learn to control our experience of it. We start by creating an EGO to help us learn to deal with these so-called same experiences. We then learn to let go of it to ensure that we are true to a final forged personality.

In this section, we will analyze how the psyche breaks free of the EGO and ends up forging a personality worthy of facing the final gate of choice.

EGO: Our Opportunity to Attempt to Fit In

Man is lonely. Man longs for a connection—the connection of knowing we are not alone as we travel on our journey of forming our personality. If travelling through hell, one could argue that being stuck there together may seem less scary than being stuck there alone. While man will always strive for a connection, he will also always thrive for acceptance and while those bound by masters thrive for recognition, the Higher Humans bound by mastery will thrive for reputation. We discussed the power of reputation earlier and its implications on our belief system and choices of direction in life. Now we will discuss its connection to our internal mastery and our ability to align our EGO with our true SELF, allowing our final personality to manifest itself.

The use of EGO has always been as a defense mechanism to allow others to come close without jeopardizing their impact on our personality or our boundaries of control. In other words, think of the EGO as a box protecting a circle within where the circle is your consciousness and the box is your vessel. While the vessel protects your psyche, the EGO protects your personality. It allows you to shape a new personality that enables a connection to others while preventing your real personality from sustaining any damage.

As many of us have experienced in any level of relationship, our connections are always more superficial and fake in the earlier stages and our trust over time enables us to let go of some of our EGO and allow others to impact our personality. As this barrier breaks, the personality becomes vulnerable to change. This change can be so powerful that it can alter so many aspects of who we are, the direction we take, our belief system, our boundary of control, and so much more. This is partly why we are warned of being careful of who we let into our circle as the creation of the EGO and its manipulation is unconscious for the masses. We form EGO to be accepted, to be allowed in, but often do not form EGO to protect ourselves from whom we let in.

The Higher Man has the ability to create and destroy his EGO on a continuous basis, over and over on a conscious basis, to program the architecture of the mastery he seeks. The common man, however, is vulnerable to being manipulated into yet another boundary of control by letting people past their EGO.

As we learned earlier, EGO can become a second personality if not carefully used. One that is accepted, loved and the personality that we wish we held. We have seen this be the case much more with people today being willing to appear to be who they want on social media rather than working on actually becoming who they believe they should be. We aren't afraid of conflict when we are behind a screen, so it allows us to put ourselves into a state of risk that wouldn't exist otherwise.

The personality is afraid of the disconnect that conflicts create, so it avoids conflict. The Higher Man, in his quest to forge a personality, understands that **conflict is simply an act in which a resolution leads to a higher state of mastery and perspective.**

The ultimate conflict for man is the constant pursuit of his personal truth, which is his own understanding and acceptance of his existence. When progress doesn't exist in this realm, he will default to the personality that allows him the feeling of progress despite not actual progressing. As a result, he forms an EGO that is more comfortable to deal with than the actual SELF, which falls short of meeting self-belief. One must accept that the forming of a personality is what holds the power of real choice, not formed in acceptance of others but formed in acceptance of the SELF and its imprint of reputation.

The issue with adding a personality to the EGO instead of the SELF is that we tend to then only focus on that which makes us feel good, be accepted, etc. We forge a personality that is bound to our EGO rather than ourselves. So often, the EGO focuses on the short-term gains, instant gratifications, and continuous levels of deceit, like distractions. It then can never give way to the greatest aspirations of the personality to be formed. This personality is one that we cannot carry with us onward through the fourth dimension, but one that keeps us tied to the third dimension, where we believe to exist rather than live.

Forged Personality: The SELF That Needs No Vessel

What is our perception of reality but the acceptance of the reflection of our image in other's eyes? For the longest time, man has longed for acceptance and created an EGO to allow himself the power of acceptance without judgment. Now, the time has come for man to forfeit his EGO and return to his SELF.

In order to understand this important journey of theological evolution, man must be willing to see himself and identify his real personality through the experience of life while he undertakes and pursues the highest levels of aspiration.

Since time is an opportunity to experience, then life on this earth isn't based on figuring out what to do or the direction to take as much as it is about allowing the experiences that we undertake to shape our personalities. A forged personality is one that is attached to the psyche. This personality is not to be confused with the vessel that allows you to carry it forward through each new state of dimensional consciousness, rather than shedding it in hopes of forming a new and improved one while staying stuck at the same level, where you are bound to the rules of existence rather than those of evolution.

This is one of the key reasons real happiness is directly linked to the progress man makes towards the meaning of his existence and not the accumulation of wealth or materialism. While both of those things can be used to ignite or maintain a state of Roush and create a marker for progress, they are an opportunity to measure progress in a societal state that is limited by the masters whom we choose to serve blindly or consciously. The real and lasting progress man seeks is the one founded on the progress of his psyche, not his vessel, bound by the opportunity to attempt to forge a personality that will transcend his time here. He will be allowed to advance to a state of fourth-dimensional awareness where one no longer needs a vessel and is no longer a prisoner to the boundary of time.

Passage: The Ability to Answer for How We Experienced Our Choices

Every day, each of us is tested by our ability to make choices, some more difficult than others. While we attempt to make what we define as the right choices for ourselves, we tend to think of each choice as an absolute. As we discussed earlier, choice is not based on absolutes and isn't defined by right or wrong. Choice is the ability to experience a direction. Often, we may define that experience as positive or negative. In the end, it's an experience, one that enables us to understand how to make future choices that are better aligned with the experiences we seek to explore in our limited time in our vessels.

While logically you may feel that making the more pleasurable choices in life would lead to a better overall lived life, do not forget that the idea of experience in itself isn't to be defined by the ease or comfort you seek, but the opportunity to forge a final personality through expansion, one that you will carry on past your existing level of dimensional awareness.

This leads us to the Gate of Choice.

The opportunity to make choices not based on pleasure, comfort, right or wrong, but on fourth-dimensional awareness. It is formed on the understanding that while our vessel is limited to experiencing life one second at a time through the arrow of time, our psyche isn't. Therefore, we define our choices by the mastery of time, not the boundary of time of it—the mastery of *how* we experience, not *what* we experience.

If the timeline of our existence has already taken its time in space, then we must accept that the experiences of pleasure, loss, sadness, and death we experience are inevitable. We must not dwell on them, but learn to craft our emotional responses to them, not allowing them to hinder our own purpose, existence, and growth. It is only then that man no longer fears time but accepts its most powerful and precious lessons. Then we can answer to ourselves, not for what we have done in this lifetime, but what we have experienced. We will discover if we have indeed mastered the choice of how we lived in our particular karmic path.

At the end of every cycle of life, one is faced with an opportunity, the opportunity to answer for their choices of how they handled their experiences in this lifetime, and to define whether such choices were based on reputation or on fear and ego. In that moment, we are given the opportunity to carry our personality onward or a chance to go back and reattempt living in a vessel for another opportunity to reestablish a better personality (also known as reliving your karmic path).

With each karmic path comes an opportunity at mastering yet another life lesson and forging yet another aspect of our personalities. With enough paths mastered and enough experiences under our belt, we can then be given the choice to move on past our three-dimensional state. While living in a four-dimensional state may be believed to be alien or science fiction, I promise you that it isn't. This dimension is simply the ability to exist in a universe no longer trapped by time, but rather one where you are in control of it, no longer limited by the boundaries of physical existence, but a simple evolution from the state you live in currently.

Think of it as no different than a snail not realizing what a dog is, or a dog not having a notion of time. A human can neither see his future shape nor understand his future boundaries of existence. He can, however, understand the components that allow him to evolve to a new state of being and understand his purpose for the present. While some men expect their purpose to expose itself to them, others seek the mastery that will allow them the power of theological evolution.

Man isn't defined by the accumulation of his wealth nor is his happiness bound the by things he acquires, but by the progress he makes. This reality is why progressing past his own physical existence is man's ultimate purpose, to return to the source you could say. His ability to overcome his existence and move to the next phase of his theological evolution, and to break free of the only boundary that he has truly been given from the beginning of his existence on earth:

The Boundary of TIME.

When man sheds this final boundary, he is given the power to reshape and reorganize his control of time, and as a result will no longer exist within its control but rather be in control of it.

Section 2:
The Path to Consciousness

Consciousness: The Opportunity to Connect All Things

Being conscious means more than to be self-aware; it means to live in a world where the self doesn't hide from its shadow.

Maslow said that consciousness would occur when a person reaches a level of self-actualization. I would agree that consciousness is possible at the stage where self- actualization begins, but I will argue that reaching that stage is only the very beginning of the first stage of consciousness. It is no different than the vessel and mind. The psyche has its own journey of learning. It starts at a stage when the vessel realizes it is, in fact, a vessel. The psyche realizes its separation from such vessel and seeks its own answers, not in the physical realm but from a state of spirituality not bound by time or fear. While each journey is bound to each soul, the process to go from a state of awareness to self-awareness to the awakening of the consciousness is a very linear process.

An evolutionary process is driven by a process of learning and advancement.

- **Man overcomes circumstance** by no longer allowing himself to be a victim of his environment. He takes control of the direction of his life and sets a destination not bound by the opinion or condition of his current environment. As a result, man is awarded ***the birth of his awareness.***

- **Man overcomes society** and no longer allows masters to dictate the rate of his growth or the direction of his learning. Man understands money and its function in the societal realm, yet its disconnect from life itself and one's reputation. As a result, man is awarded the opportunity to recognize the "I" (SELF) from the "WE" and ***becomes self-aware***.

- **Man masters society** when he no longer associates his rank under the umbrella of a master and has earned his freedom from the barriers of fear. When man succeeds monetarily, he earns his time freedom back from masters and takes on the opportunity to spend his time as he pleases. For this mastery, man is awarded ***the opportunity to start on the path of self-actualization*** (the beginning of fourth-dimensional consciousness).

- **Man commits to excellence and creativity** and holds no boundaries to society, its core possibilities, and expectation. Instead, he conquers his fears of judgment and focuses on his craft, giving ***his life direction and, more importantly, "meaning".***

- **Man overcomes his EGO** in his quest for meaning. He learns to shed the personality he formed to get himself to this point of his conscious journey, understanding that he no longer cares for the perception of others, but rather seeks his own experience to create his own truth. Giving life to a real personality, ***he finally awakens the SELF and actualizes.***

- **Man masters aspiration,** in order to push the boundaries of his third-dimensional existence and understands his separation from the fourth. He is no longer bound by the shadows that prevent him but by the light that powers him. Man now no longer lives for himself, but rather ***for the capacity of his imprint and reputation.***

- **Man forges a personality**, one formed from his aspiration and forged by his reputation, one where he accepts his role in the bigger picture of life, not in this realm but in all realms. He is no longer afraid of shadows and EGO, no longer bound to masters, and no longer constrained by fear. ***Man has finally awakened his full consciousness and is ready to face the Gate of Choice.***

For the longest time, man has lost his way. He has renounced his true SELF in exchange for his EGO. Today, man must relearn not just to be free, but also to be one with his true SELF.

In this next section, we will examine the baseline for how man has enslaved himself, what he must do to set himself free, and also how to use the basic functions available to us in order to live a more fulfilling life that is focused on reaching a higher state of consciousness, one ready to face the Gate of Choice.

Expectations: A Creation of Boundaries

We discussed the dangers of being bound to masters instead of committing to mastery. Part of the reason we gravitate towards masters is that we ourselves constantly create boundaries internally. These boundaries are what we refer to as "expectations". While having high expectations of one's self is very much a necessity when evolving, one expectation of their environment is what becomes a never-ending trap.

Man should expect excellence of himself but should not have expectations of excellence from his environment or those that exist within it. When our expectations are set that are out of our control, we tend to then set boundaries in our thinking by caging ourselves to a predestined set of behaviors and outlook that makes us form our own internal boundary of action. We reduce our possible life directions out of fear, even though it isn't necessary. This may sound complicated, but in the real world, it is very easy to see.

Let's take our viewpoint on Corporate America. Once we expect (or force) Corporate America to be the one to create income equality, we create a sense of victimhood that cages our behavior. We become ones who cannot attain a state of financial freedom for ourselves and must rely on others to level out the playing field in get in the game.

An entry-level job with a minimum wage isn't there to provide enough to live. It is simply there to present the opportunity to enter the workforce, learn skills, and advance, even if not within the same company. Once we attain such employment, the mind tends to slow down its desire to grow and quickly conforms to a life that meets the pay received.

Instead of quickly attempting to rise past the pay, the person reorganizes their expectation around the pay, then setting the expectation that such pay is now standard. While the cost of living rises, one expects their pay to rise with it. Over time, when it doesn't increase, one turns to others to fix this inequity, as they feel cheated or their survival is at risk.

In reality, from the very beginning, one could have used the initial pay as leverage to learn more skills, try harder, and suffer through the basics of learning life. Instead, an expectation has been set that, for the minimal pay received, minimal effort will be made, since the job is what is believed to be replaceable. Once that belief is accepted, it should also be accepted that we, as individuals, are replaceable and therefore the boundary of self-induced fear is assigned on the basis that our survival is now in the hands of others.

This combination of expectations creates a non-evolutionary environment where mastery is now replaced with a master, one created from the expectation to not evolve but conform. We then play victim to the advancement of a corporation that is constantly adapting, blaming those at the top for why the roles at the bottom are not increasing despite the increase in business.

These roles are actually decreasing in value, forcing the basic labor force into subpar living wages. During such moments, the mind of those bound to masters chooses to blame others for the changes that have occurred rather than the SELF for the lack of change or advancement. We blame CEOs for not valuing labor when we should blame ourselves for not learning new skills and advancing to non-labor work. The choice in the acceptance of the failed process is either defined by our belief in our masters or our acceptance of our lack of mastery.

We can look at similar issues as they pertain to the education system as well. We expect formal education to provide an opportunity to become successful in society, although the definition of success differs from one person to the next. A common denominator in belief is that the further your formal education has been explored, the more money you will make, which in many cases, isn't true. It is simply an expectation built off of the external marketing by the universities who need your money as revenue, not based on reality. We can certainly blame the school system for marketing the possibility of success, but we should also blame ourselves for accepting that marketing to be the ultimate savior, rather than investigating the path we seek. I have met many young people with degrees in studies that would be obsolete in ten years. Yet they are expected to graduate in four. When asked about their industry's future, many simply have no knowledge or idea of any of the possibilities or changes their industry faces.

By the time they actually graduate, they will no longer hold an opportunity to exercise what they have learned in school. They instead wait around expecting the education system to make that shift and provide such information and knowledge for them. In reality, all of this information has been available for all of them to discover on their own. Once again, we see another clear example of how expectation creates a boundary of fear, which once again passes the control of our lives away from mastery and into the shadows of a master.

Here is yet another way to see this. We look to fairness and equality from a government with the expectation that the role of the government is to enable its population to prosper and grow. We feel cheated when we realize that the balance of fairness is not tilted in our favor. Rather than blaming ourselves for not learning to play the game or to make the money by taking 20 years to make a name for ourselves, we believe it is the government's priority—not our own—to create a fair playing field for us to play on.

This fear and resentment towards a pre-set expectation pushes us away from the entire concept as a whole, now giving further excuses why we will not vote, take part in paying taxes, or try to fit in society. We believe the system is rigged, and as a result, allow this pre-determined expectation stemming from a single disappointment to dictate the boundary of control once more set by others.

We blame our failure on the uncontrollable actions of others based on the wrong expectations; however, if our expectation from the beginning was that government was never meant to help us prosper but simply enable population control, to ensure new baselines are available to make sure the population doesn't outgrow the system in place to maintain it, then we would never blame "IT" for our failures towards a prosperous life. Instead, from the very beginning, we would have never relied on its fairness or balance.

The issue here is not to reduce expectations of one's self. The logic becomes flawed when we expect of others and believe that our perspective of truth is the same as everyone else's universal truth. When we do so, we create a boundary of truth based on a limited perspective that is geared to benefit us. If such benefit doesn't occur, we once more fall victim to defining our own evolution by the baseline of right or wrong, good or bad, which enables our inclusion into the Herd, negating the ability to grow and make progress towards the Superman.

Happiness: Progress Toward Meaning

Ask the average man what he seeks in life, and he will answer in a word that he himself cannot define: Happiness.

There are so many always seek to be happy, yet so few people can articulate what happiness means to them. A large obstacle to evolution facing man today is his inability to see life through an evolutionary state of awareness.

Man must learn to find his answers, learning from his past rather than questioning his future. That, in itself, is the definition of growth and evolution.

“What has made me happy so far?”

This question seeks a pattern to replicate, learn from, and advance to.

“How do I achieve lasting happiness?”

This question shows doubt and the inability to piggyback off past learning.

It is in the simplicity of the perspective that man can find many of the difficult answers to life. A simple tweak of time (fourth-dimensional thinking) on the same question produces two very different answers, opening the opportunity for deeper and more thoughtful answers to hold ourselves accountable to.

It is because in a way man is afraid of the answers that he will have to face within himself by asking such questions.

After all, man’s greatest fears are based on the possibilities of the unknown. Holding the answers to one’s internal question requires one to follow through into the unknown in the quest for progress.

It is only when man makes progress that he realizes that, with each step forward, he gains tremendous knowledge, awareness, and wisdom. He then becomes attached to his evolution, rather than his contempt. In this state of enlightenment, man no longer attached to his third-dimensional state and possessions but rather his fourth-dimensional evolution, enabling the progress he makes to become his state of happiness.

While many on the outside may see progress in the physical realm and identify items like cars, homes, planes, or other materialism as the source of one's happiness, they will also miss that the internal journey one goes through requires an elevated mindset that is committed to excellence and creativity, as stated earlier in this book. Such commitment is often rewarded with wealth. As a result, this wealth may seem to have been the basis for the happiness when in reality it is only the by-product of it.

This poses the basic question: Is money directly tied to happiness?

To understand the answer, one must frame the understanding of both money and happiness. Money is nothing more than an exchange of value from a party that has nothing to offer but currency, to gain access to the value you provide. **The more committed you are to excellence and creativity, the more others will value the services or products you provide** them and will exchange their money for your value. While money (a tangible third-dimensional item) cannot directly buy happiness (a feeling), it can become a bridge to facilitating it.

Lasting happiness doesn't come from the acquisition of things, but certainly doesn't come from ignoring them either. While many will say that true happiness comes from health and family, it is equally untrue, just as to the idea that it comes from money. Lasting happiness comes from one's ability to advance, to find progress towards their meaning. The more progress one makes, the more happiness they live with.

If one associates progress with more wealth, then a sense of happiness exists by accumulating more things. If one associates life's meaning with family, then the more health and growth their family experiences, the happier they are. Both of these scenarios can be considered accurate ways to achieve more happiness, depending on your perspective, but both are very much flawed.

If money is the indicator, then at times when you no longer can or want to upgrade your life, you will feel a void. You find yourself going to a state of no purpose, something that happens too often to those stuck in the prison of society that defines success only by your monetary capacity.

The same can be said for family. If we have a large family or create one, our role in such family is clearly defined (like the mom or dad). As a result, we find a sense of purpose. As the dynamics change—such as kids getting older, moving out, or marriages falling apart—we lose our sense of purpose because we no longer can move towards this false assignment that we had given ourselves as our life purpose.

A journey based on the accumulation of wealth is as equally flawed as a journey based on the fostering of a family.

Both of those perspectives are escapes from the inability to actually escape the box of fear we do not want to be trapped in. The connection between the two may be the ultimate victory in life, but I would argue that it couldn't be farther from the truth.

Man's vessel was never created to simply create more vessels, nor was he created to accumulate wealth. If we learned anything from the first part of this book, man's ultimate role is to forge a personality. All such experiences, such as family and wealth, are an opportunity to learn how to deal with certain experiences that come with them. As a result, man gains a higher level of wisdom through his third-dimensional existence for an opportunity to define what side of choice he will stand on when faced with the Gate of Choice in the next phase of his journey.

It is only when man finds his happiness directly correlated to the progress that he makes towards this specific meaning that man will find that happiness can not only become everlasting but also no longer use third-dimensional experiences to prevent himself from facing his fourth-dimensional evolution.

Chakras: A Tool to Conduct Energy

Many speak of the energies that constantly surround us, from one's connection to the universe to harvesting energy. One must learn that energy is the essence of what we define as the universe, and that the reason we can receive and give out energy is that all things are connected with purpose on a dimensional level.

Humans connect with other humans, and animals with other animals. While the two can also cross connect, the connection isn't based on a common understanding but rather co-existence in each energy source's purpose.

This phenomenon occurs around us at all times. While some of us attempt to harness energy, we must learn to let go of the idea that energy is there for us to take. Energy exists for us to tap into. It's like the relationship you have with water, not from a possessive standpoint but your ability to take in water as needed, only to let it flow through your body and eventually leave. **There is** really **no state at which you retain all the energy** or water **you gain. Instead, you learn to make it part of everything you do, allowing the energy to flow through you.**

When man is born, he is a body of energy, that energy is trapped in seven chakras that align from the top of the head to the bottom of the toes. These chakras control the flow of your energy. Think of them as the organs of your psyche, similar to the organs of your body. Your mind becomes the connection between such energy and the body that protects them. How your mind interprets information enables or disables the flow of energy.

Imagine you suffer massive trauma in your early childhood with regard to love. The mind will create a layer of EGO around the heart chakra, preventing it from expanding or receiving any more energy. It does so to protect its existence and to prevent the pain you fear. Therefore, the fear creates a box that prevents the heart from functioning in synchronicity with the other energy centers in your body. The same can happen to any of your chakras. Your fear of your sexuality and confidence in your design, for example, make it hard for you to share a state of connection with others through sex because you fear judgment, creating a barrier that prevents you from having a real connection in bed with someone.

This happens a lot to people who separate sex from love, as an example. They possess the ability to consciously or subconsciously prevent the flow of energy from the heart to the crotch area. While your chakras may be an energy source you cannot visually see, it is force you certainly can feel as long as you are able to hold a state of self-awareness, one where you are not afraid of who you see in a mirror. One where you can face your own shortcomings and realize the power of allowing a flow of energy through all your chakras and body without restriction.

It is only then that man realizes that the seven chakras were never meant to capture energy but to enable the flow of energy through the body, similar to the veins your blood flows through. Imagine how much damage would occur to any part of your body that doesn't allow a proper flow. Now imagine how much of your psyche is damaged by blocking the energy flow.

Understanding the seven chakras is simple. The connection to the physical is what enables you to understand how much is actually connected to the mind and its perception of your existence in time. Remember that all humans are nothing than four-dimensional beings trapped in a three-dimensional box. Therefore, when you learn to connect the two and break free of the EGO, you discover the SELF. When you discover the SELF, you open up the opportunity to understand how to live free of the box they have been made to worship.

More importantly, one understands the connection of the psyche to time, the only box we will forever be chained to in our current form.

You can open the seven chakras by understanding their connection.

Crown: Your earned opportunity to finally own the SELF

Third Eye: Your ability to interpret your intuition

Throat: Your ability to vocalize without fear

Heart: Love for yourself

Solar: Confidence and belief

Sacral: Your sexuality and emotional strength

Root: Your grounding and ability to secure your own your safety

If we align these to the Maslow's hierarchy of needs, we realize that all the theories of evolution point back to the exact same evolutionary patterns, even if at times described with other words.

These are just different ways to show that each and every human has the same path to the discovery of the SELF and its theological evolution. We can combine chakras together to reflect each of the sections found in Maslow's theories. The same connection can be made to *Third Circle Theory* and just about all other theories on evolution.

The point is that the universe and its energies are there to be tapped into by the Higher Man. We harness energy that we convert in our minds to the will to power, but we also must learn to let the energy flow through the rest of our bodies. We do this by constantly monitoring and preventing our mind from sheltering each chakra with its own EGO—a layer of protection that the mind deems necessary to protect the chakra from suffering any permanent damage. The EGO also shields our inability to face ourselves, based on the pain of allowing the energy flow through.

In simple terms, we could say that we close our hearts to pain instead of learning to flow through pain.

When we experience pain in our heart, we reject any future feeling of such, like riding a bike as a child is terrifying if the pain of the fall is still on your mind. We must let go of this idea that it is best to go through life sheltered from the experiences that lead to pain. We often make this mistake by assigning energy a value of pleasure or pain, good or bad. Instead, **we should understand that energy is meant to be understood, felt, and synchronized with—not rejected or accepted—even if, at times, the energy isn't pleasurable.**

This pain is experienced from a state of unknown, a state where the psyche is shocked, not hurt. It is here that we escape behind the idea of allowing masters to create boxes in which we feel safe rather than capable. These boxes of comfort feed our fears of the experience and force us to a state of constant worship. Within these boxes, we give up our evolution towards earning our crown and regulating the energies of our lives. Instead, we remain a state rooted in comfort and safety.

Simplicity: The Solution to a Difficult Life

Since time is the ultimate boundary of control, man is fearful of losing any of it. For that reason, **man is divided between his fear of living a life of no guarantees and his fear of missing out on his own pleasure.** It is only a matter of understanding that both of these fears relate to the passiveness of time. The simple fact is that a timeline once lived cannot be re-experienced. Therefore, time limits us to the basic concept of choice once more, the basic choice of WHAT we choose to experience.

Do we want to experience the possibility of finding meaning and purpose or the guarantee of living through pleasure? This very basic choice comes back to how one finds his own state of happiness.

I would rather live an entire lifetime fighting for purpose, rather than one settled for pleasure.

Perhaps the answer doesn't lie in the belief but rather in the expectation we have come to have of life—an expectation skewed by masters who have trapped us in a box that required obedience rather than meaning.

Perhaps, we have come to expect life to be easy, when in itself, **it is in the difficulties that man has always found his deepest SELF** and removed his EGO. Easy was never really part of the journey. Instead, over the years, masters have made it easy for men to give up their suffering and relinquish control of their time in exchange for pleasure.

When man is faced with discomfort and suffering, he often chooses to retract and find refuge in the calm. However, man is always given an opportunity to face the storm. Choose to not run away into a state of comfort but realize how to create a sense of stability and calm within the storm itself. Don't ignore that the idea of chaos is inevitable and that, in order to no longer live or experience a state of suffering, you must be willing to progress through the suffering rather than avoid it.

Most of man's aspirations have always been within reach. While man has been divided by the idea that institution and life hold two separate meanings, he has also been given the opportunity to progress through both by understanding their respective roles.

Think of everything you want: money, love, success, fame, etc. Then think of everything in the way of your goal. **It is often your fear that is the only barrier between you and everything you want.**

Think about the simplest of concepts, the idea of being wealthy. *There are thousands of ways to make money in this world. Yet, man finds the one reason to not try.*

Think about love. *There are thousands of ways for man to love and be loved, but yet he sees the one for why he cannot be loved.*

Often man complicates his own life by adding this layer of fear. He confuses easy with simple, assuming that all simple tasks are easy or that all easy tasks are simple. While simple tasks may seem physically easy, the difficulty lies in the psyche and the overcoming of one's own fear and boundary of control.

Asking a woman out on a date is a simple task. Walk up to someone you are attracted to and ask. The complication of this simple act comes in the FEAR that exists with the outcome. The inability to deal with the possibility of the outcome and its aftermath prompts one to forfeit the attempt and label it as difficult.

The same occurs with fostering creativity and selling such through a business. An artist creates a painting through his inspiration, but fears offering it for sale. The act of creation, which is the hardest part, is met with belief and ease. The transaction then—equally simple in its physical form—is met with doubt and fear, making the process extremely difficult.

We must learn to no longer look through the lens of fear but rather understand that **many of the most difficult tasks in life are only made difficult by the fear that comes between the thought and act itself.** While letting go of fear isn't easy, it is also very simple. Instead of fearing something that has yet to take place, we should choose to believe that we can shape an experience driven by light—not to allow our shadow to be the default setting of the events we fear to experience. All of this once more comes down to how we love ourselves.

Love: The Opportunity to Love One's Self

A man once told me that everything is LOVE and that love conquers all, but he himself didn't even understand what love meant.

Over the last few generations, the idea of love has been associated with a relationship, one that often requires another person. We love our parents, we love our significant others, we love new people we meet, but in the majority of cases, we love only for the purpose of being loved back. The reason is partially because we never really loved ourselves. And yet **we expected others to love us for who we are, even though we didn't even accept that who we are is someone worth loving.**

Man lost his sense of love when he no longer saw in the mirror the power to become the person he was once meant to become. He lost his touch with his true SELF and created an EGO that he expected others to love so that he would never have to fix himself.

While he loved, only to know how it would feel to be loved back, he forgot that true love isn't based on a relationship with others. It is an opportunity to love the true SELF and its becoming. Loving not what others expect you to love, but rather loving the true personality you created, and allowing it to shape a body and character worthy of your own love.

While most love only to know the feeling of being loved or the feeling of acceptance, the Higher Man loves himself as a reflection of being all he can be. A love that isn't judged by the Herd or the masses in society, but a love for one's SELF is linked directly to the evolution of himself towards his meaning. A man who doesn't believe in himself and doesn't love himself cannot truly know how to love others, as he cannot actually know who others are.

So how can man get closer to loving himself?

As discussed earlier, recognizing the difference between the EGO and the SELF is the first opportunity man has to align who he is and to allow his life to have a greater sense of meaning. Only then, he must make progress towards that meaning and not fall in love with the meaning itself. He must give worth and love to himself, based on the character and personality he is developing that allows him to make such progress. It is only then that man will truly develop an inner sense of love for himself, rather than love for the hope of acceptance and for an opportunity to be loved.

The evolution of Inner Love for man is broken down into this very simple transition as he evolves into a higher sense of dimensional awareness.

Align Lifestyle to Value.

Align Value to Meaning

Align Meaning to Character.

Align Character to SELF.

Align SELF to Personality.

Allow Love to foster for the Personality.

Allow Love to flow freely between the SELF and the Personality.

By adopting this basic understanding, man replaces the EGO with the personality. In this way, he allows the personality to become the protector from those who only love us to be loved. This enables the experience of love itself to not be kept from taking its course in our life. Instead, we have a filter that only allows those who truly love us for who we are, not for how we love them to get close to our SELF.

One of the easiest ways to decipher one from the other is in the language of how we love. Pay attention to why people act in loving ways in society. We can simply ask people who are in relationships why they love those whom they claim to love. The majority of people will simply state that they love "how someone makes them laugh" rather than say "because they are funny" or "he allows me to be free or myself" rather than "he is true to himself". One statement makes it about ourselves, while the other is a testament to that person. All of this language is meant to satisfy our lack of love for ourselves rather than loving for who the SELF is.

We can determine that by the flow of language. Is it unconscious and focused on the person's own feelings even though the question is guided to another person's personality? For example, "I love him because he makes me laugh" is simply a statement saying that I love that person because of how their actions impact my feelings and well-being, not a personality trait of theirs.

You may look at this from the lens that we are simply dissecting a sentence that technically means the same thing. We are really looking more closely at your love for yourself. Does it exist as a means of deciphering those who understand that love is a state of being? One cannot be in such state when unaware of who they are. Love is a powerful state of being that enables us to connect to each other in a fourth-dimensional state, even past the vessel's existence. Love plays a vital role in the contracts we form in between such dimensions.

In order to evolve, one must shed the need to be loved and instead learn how to love one's self. When one knows how to love one's self, one knows how to stand in their light facing their shadows and as a result can show love towards others.

Light: The Strength to Look Into Your Own Shadows

Man is bound by masters. He has often recognized life as a means of worshiping God and rejecting Satan, two figures often associated with good versus evil. Pushing on the idea that giving in to evil would result in an afterlife in hell while giving yourself to God would result in a pleasant trip to heaven. While religion does its best to be a be a boundary of control for man, it is the perversion of those who have used structure not to allow the evolution of man, but rather its obedience.

Since man is bound by many boxes during his quest to cultivate his personality, it is easy to become trapped by the *fear* of an afterlife that cannot be explained. For centuries, society has given more and more power to those who preach of knowing God's words or the afterlife of a life well-lived or ill-conceived. Society even gives a fake sense of separation of church and state when, in reality, they have simply chosen to not prosecute those who chose to not participate in church but rather regulate them through government.

What if we eliminated all these boundaries of control and instead looked at our third-dimensional experience as a balance of our light and shadows from the psyche?

What if the world wasn't constructed on good or evil? We would look at the balance of forces (light) that encourages the evolution of the psyche (soul). We distinguish from other forces (shadows) that attempt to slow it down. Since we are fourth-dimensional beings trapped in a third-dimensional state, then it would simply mean that we are learning the balance of existence at a much slower pace, allowing us to actually experience cause and effect. Next comes the ultimate question:

How would you live if you were free of judgment and prosecution?

What if you weren't judged for your actions? What if you weren't punished for your crimes? How would your behavior change?

This is a dangerous question, but certainly a necessary one to answer. If man only functions based on the boundaries of control in which he is allowed to operate, then man only learns based to function in a third-dimensional state controlled by other masters.

Think of life like you think of art.

If we only allowed artists to create from a state of guidelines, then art would never progress. It would never allow us to experience truth and perspective from the mind of an artist, as every artist's mind would be corrupted by the directions and instructions of masters who have been limited in their ability to create. The same can be said about evolution. Man cannot evolve to a higher state of being if he is confined to the same prisons (boundaries of control) as others who never will evolve.

Religions, society, government and other boundaries of control have been created to control the light and shadows that we experience. They are meant to cover up the truth, partially because an evolved state of consciousness would reveal how flawed they really are and how corrupt they have become. Instead, these ***boundaries of control offer protection from the shadows in exchange for giving up the experience of what a life in pursuit of truth really means.***

When man commits to evolving, he must then make the sacrifice of travelling through the shadows in search of the truth (his own internal light). He must travel through the shadows that he fears, not fearing judgment or to be cast as different, but accepting that creativity in itself is a man's discovery of his own truth and how he chooses to perceive the world. He must realize that his shadows are not evil, no matter how sinister or disgusting they seem to others. His shadows present an opportunity to choose how to live. He must rid himself of all elements of good or bad, and translate all aspects of life to a quest for internal truth.

During this journey, man will be ridiculed, outcast, and made to believe he is delusional for wanting to explore the shadows that lie outside of the boundaries of controls that have been set by the masters. Picture someone starting a business and being reminded that by his peers that he simply won't make it. Others fear that they will be considered cowards when one of their own faces his shadows and overcomes them. Meanwhile, these peers are stuck, afraid to face their own fears. When man overcomes this important aspect of life, he no longer fears seeing the world for what it, a constant cosmic battle of light and shadows, both internally and externally. Instead, he is able to forge his personality on the basis of the choices that he makes. He no longer turns his back to the shadows that face him with but discovers a way to bring his light into every encounter.

Man will find his light at the highest peak of his creativity, in a place where his awareness is heightened to a state of self-awareness. ***Where fears disappear, choices dominate and judgment dissipates, achieving a state where consciousness evolves, and the SELF is born.***

Choice: Man's Greatest Force Towards "Becoming"

There is no right and wrong and no good or evil. Yet, we cannot put in perspective why we seem to be pulled in two very different directions at various times. Directions that we must fundamentally declare right or wrong, according to our set of values (which are not necessarily helpful to our evolution). They were assigned to us from previous generations who suffered even more so than we have with an identity crisis—the majority of which came once more from masters and obedience rather than finding the SELF.

The pull we feel isn't an external one of morals, as we seem to believe but rather an internal one from our light and shadow. While light and shadow are opposites, they work together as man's shadow is necessary for his wholeness as much as his light. Ignoring one's shadow in hopes that the light will prevail is an illusion that associates light to good and shadow to evil.

On the other hand, the balance of this internal force needs a direction, and with this direction comes the ultimate choice:

The choice of "intention".

Not just the intention of your actions that exist within your third-dimensional state of being in the present but rather the intention of your existence, led by your fourth-dimensional SELF, the one bound to evolve.

The ultimate choice is one of intention, being, and living a life of Wisdom or Deceit.

You have the choice to live a life led by your shadow towards deceit or one led by your light towards wisdom. This is the ultimate purpose of one's life, the choice of intention that you will have to answer for at the end of each and every karmic path. Answer for whether you have truly encompassed the wisdom necessary in each third-dimensional field to forge a personality or if you fell victim to your shadow, leading your intent to live a life of self-deceit. A life whose intention wasn't to evolve or to gain wisdom but rather seek comfort and become one's master.

Choosing a life of wisdom comes through these three basic life commitments we discussed throughout section one.

Choice of excellence: To take ownership of your actions on a day-to-day basis. To commit to learning and practicing your trade, no matter what it is. To understand the power of excellence through your work, your relationships and your being. To be the best version of yourself at all times, despite being faced with circumstance, life, and hardship. A mental state where the decision is made that no average performance will ever lead to greater wisdom.

Choice of mastery: To understand that a choice of excellence followed by a state of mastery is the definition of true entrepreneurship. A skill turned into a talent, a talent turned into a gift. The gift of letting the third-dimensional world experience, the power of establishing a reputation. That to be remembered is more than to be praised for your EGO, but rather to guide others through a collective journey of knowledge, not limited by the arrow of time.

Choice of wisdom: To decide to love despite the pain, to experience despite the fear, to allow the flow of energy despite the EGO are all elements that lead to man forging a personality strong enough to withstand theological evolution, all of which are linked by man's choice to live a life connected to who he is, a life of purpose not driven by the limitation of time, but by the continuity of his learning. Such life is given meaning through the progress one makes towards acquiring the wisdom he needs with each karmic lesson he is to overcome.

At the end of each karmic path, man will be given a choice, based on his commitment to these principles of excellence, mastery, and wisdom. At this point, he will be given an opportunity to evolve or to re-experience a path in hopes of finding enough wisdom to face the SELF once more, and to forge the needed personality to evolve.

Think of this no differently from how we, as third-dimensional humans, have established our very own ecosystem of evolution through our formalized education. We undergo each school grade with an opportunity to learn a subject, a topic of behavior. With each grade, we are faced with a final test. This test is intended to identify our ability to function in the next grade.

Those of us who do not take in or accept the information we are taught are forced to repeat the process until showing a certain level of acceptance and discipline. Each grade, even if repeated, is unique, because the environment in which the education occurs differs, often with different teachers, students, and curriculums. While we may have memorized an entire year worth of content, we are forced to adapt as the final test each year differs, pushing us to embrace the understanding and not just cheat our way out of the grade.

This is the same parallel as the EGO versus SELF. Each karmic path places us in a different setting, circumstance, and ecosystem. We are forced to attempt to align ourselves rather than use our EGO to cheat out way back to the Gate. It is in this effort that we realize that true evolution isn't about advancement, but rather acceptance and growth.

An opportunity to choose Wisdom over Deceit gives us a new understanding that ***free will was never about creating our own destiny, but rather accepting how to experience it.***

Each karmic path we experience is ultimately like a school grade driven to show our capacity for existence in the fourth parallel. Our free will becomes an opportunity to experience life from a different perspective, not in the hope of survival, but in the progress of the established personality we seek to carry onward.

Free Will: The Ability to Choose Your Intent

Earlier in this book we discussed the idea that if time is relative, then someone who experiences time at a significantly faster pace than we do would have full access to our timeline. What we are to a snail, travelling significantly faster, allows us to play God or be a God-like figure to the slower creature. We can also determine that, if someone lives within a capacity to function at a significantly faster speed than us, then their existence across 10 minutes could be no different than our existence for 100 years.

This relativity is what makes me accept that, while we may have free will with how we experience things, we also could not have any control over the fourth dimension. Why are bound to the arrow of time. A fourth-dimensional being would be bound to the possible outcomes of time rather than to time itself. This is where free will can get interesting. Having the ability to make choices in experiences changes the outcomes of time for a particular being, never the actual timeline itself.

Free will is where choice comes in. While the majority of humanity makes their decisions based on factors of control in their third-dimensional states, the Higher Man learns to make decisions while taking in consideration "the echo of time".

The echo of time reflects that one decision will have an infinite effect on one's timeline, beyond its third-dimensional existence. **When we consider that our decisions matter beyond ourselves, we reflect on the intent of such decisions,** starting with the beginning of our intent towards ourselves to the effects such decisions have on others.

We discussed this briefly earlier when we looked at cause and effect. We determined that cause and effect can only be taken in as a possibility if we examine each through the lens of time and the chain reaction of events that led to the core event. We cannot simply say, "X happened which caused Y", without understanding the relevance of what led to X.

Think about a decision, such as smoking, and its adverse effects on your body. There is no longer any doubt that smoking has negative effects on the body. There is no wisdom to such act but deceit. The inability for one to cope with stress forces a behavior to escape *the inability to create a solution*, which gives temporary release but at a cost. The cost is losing a perfectly healthy vessel and damaging other's vessels, and, more importantly, living in the fear of not dealing with the circumstance that causes the stress to begin with.

While this temporary solution addresses one's inability to function, it certainly doesn't fix the issue at hand. It creates a much larger problem in the echo of time. The same can be said with alcohol and one's inability to function within a social place, reflecting the need to be put in state of comfort over being in a state of confidence. These very basic examples can be applied to a much more severe decision, like choosing to stay in a job we hate that discourages wisdom for the moment, because it creates a state of comfort and forces us to avoid the discomfort that seeking excellence and mastery provide in a new field.

While we may justify such an act with the simple notion of survival, man was never made to survive; man was created to evolve. The simple opportunity to make a decision to work at a job where we can grow or to take on entrepreneurship is then justified by the deceit that we are making the best decision towards our family's survival. In reality, at any given time, we could simply seek better employment. Life doesn't take place in the absolute of do's and don'ts, but instead deceives us by creating fake limitations derived from the fear of facing our lack of skills, lack of confidence, and rejection.

We continue the deceit by justifying our comfort over our evolution. The same exact scenario can be related to parents who deceive themselves by believing their purpose was to be mothers and fathers, choosing to not face the reality that they have given up on their own beliefs and progress.

The underlying premise here is to understand that the power of choice (free will) comes with the opportunity to hold the correct intent towards this third-dimensional journey of growth, and not fall victim to self-deceit. We have the capacity to not run away from the experiences that life brings and to face our greatest shadows, regardless of the pain that the choice brings. The ability to live a life driven forward by the intent of wisdom, not deceit. By doing so, we are offered the idea of evolving from the higher man to *"The Superman."*

Section 3: The Bridge, The Gate, The Choice, The Superman

In this final section, we will explore the path of man from the final stage of consciousness in the third dimension to the birth of his own fourth-dimensional SELF. Humanity has made a fundamental mistake in its evolution is its misunderstanding of what it means to exist. Man has chosen to pollute the universe with its selfish desire to stay here in our third-dimensional form rather than evolve. Once such a mistake was made, many forms of fourth-dimensional beings (referred to as "biblical figures" in today's society) attempted to set us back on our path only to be met with deceit and ridicule.

Individuals who came to us in hopes of providing the benefit of us to choose a path of wisdom and evolution were made to become martyrs, used by other masters for the purpose of deceit and control. Each time such a being made an appearance on Earth, man had an opportunity to learn and grow, but more importantly, to overcome himself and his greatest aspirations. Fueled by contempt in the comfort of their masters, the majority of man chose the way of Last Human—a man so lost in his own distraction that he has given up on his highest hopes.

These forces that govern our timelines are here now as observers and attempting one last time to remind us of the consequences of ignoring our fundamental purpose as humans "to evolve and overcome."

Choosing to ignore our fundamental destiny as a race could mean meeting once more the same faith that many civilizations before us faced: "extinction."

Destiny Theory: The Opportunity to Become

We discussed the power of understanding our souls as circles, capable of expanding and retracting, with no beginning and no end. When one accepts life with a sense of continuity, one can start to realize that reputation and overcoming play a major factor in their evolution. Now imagine a perfect circle, one that is geometrically as perfectly round as possible, drawn with a tool to allow no imperfections in its radius. Pick a point on top of the circle and establish a starting point for your pencil.

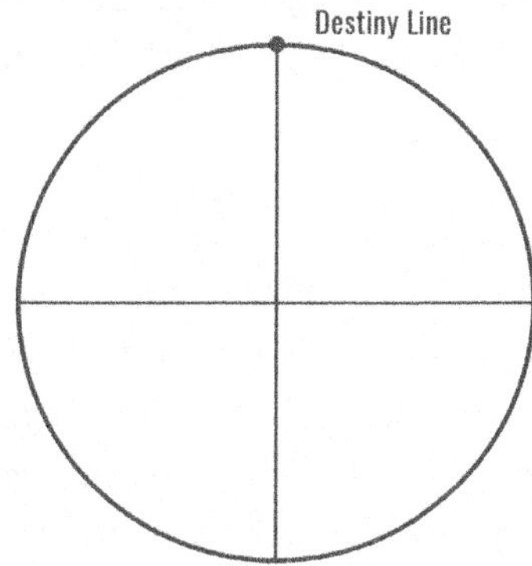

Now attempt to draw on top of the circle by hand. You can only move your pencil clockwise, never going back, just like your experience of time.

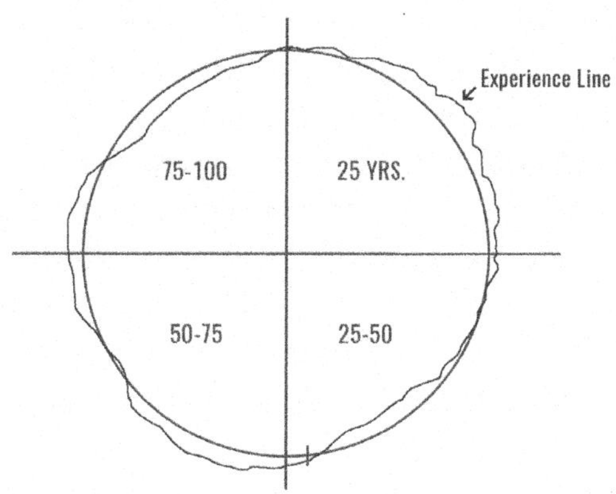

You will realize that at various stages of your life, the pencil will or will not stay true to the perfect circle. At times the line will venture away from the circle, and at times, inside of it. Depending on your age, your skills, your steadiness, and your capacity, the circle you draw will be far from perfect, yet its end point will be exactly the same as its starting point.

The farther out of the circle you venture, the more that shadow consumes you. The more inwards you travel, the more that comfort protects you. This isn't a game of light and darkness, but rather man's ability to understand that time cannot run backwards and to accept that **while, at some points and times in life we find ourselves going towards masters or mastery, we always retain the ability to get centered once more and come back to our balance point.**

The balance point is the place where we do not fear the experiences in front of us. Here, we understand that the entire purpose of having already lived a lifetime without yet having experienced it is to overcome the experience, rather than question the reasoning it happens. You may not understand why one's innocent children are taken away, or why someone's beloved mother must leave before she has completed a full life cycle. The reasoning is irrelevant. What is relevant is the impact of such experiences on the soul and its ability to overcome them.

Think about a disgusting act of terrorism, like the one we described previously, or someone being raped and violated. There is no justifiable reason that makes the act acceptable from the standpoint of right or wrong. In every way, the act itself is very deceitful towards those involved and those committing it. While the action it is one very few can accept, all those involved will have to overcome its experiences, regardless of whether one can understand why someone would do that. Many seek justice and revenge on those committing the act, but never overcome the experience itself. They think that the experience makes them a victim of life rather than giving them a chance to learn how to once more overcome the experience itself.

Many will argue that life isn't always black and white. I would argue that a perfect circle on a page is black and white. The journey of those attempting to draw their own circle as close to that perfect version of themselves is very much in the grey area. This inability to pursue a perfect version of one's SELF is how man finds himself trapped in a state of stagnancy rather than a state of evolution. This is because man is no longer living his life but unquestionably accepting the experiences that his EGO has created for him.

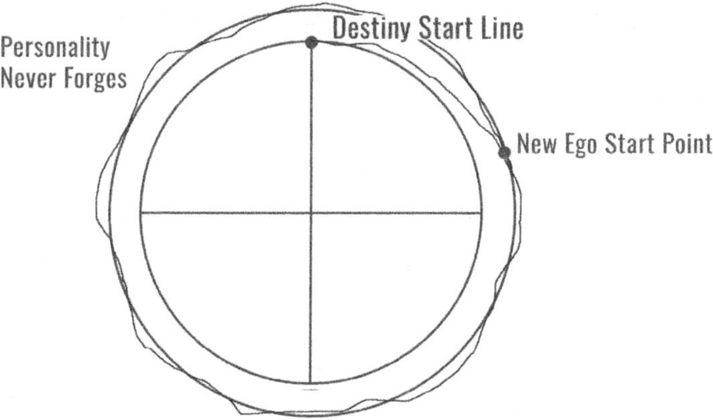

Take him away from his destiny and into his need for comfort and protection. While protection from the EGO is necessary for the psyche to survive society as a whole, it is the most dangerous aspect of diverging from the experience we are intent on overcoming. It's no different than cheating our way to the completion of a video game, rather than learning the skills to becoming the person ready to take on the following stage and challenges we face. This is also why instant gratification is often found in the minds of those who live through their EGO, not their true SELF.

If you recall the evolution of man through the Third Circle, then you remember that man first overcomes his circumstance, then society, and then life. One of the flaws in evolution is our inability to connect information early on as our awareness and self-awareness hasn't evolved enough. For this reason, why you may have found new knowledge in *Third Circle*

Theory today that didn't exist when you first opened its pages back in 2013.

Your awareness allows you to accept information differently at various stages of your life. In other words, each time you read the concept, a new person accepts its information. Your evolution dictates your understanding. One of the hidden concepts of *Third Circle Theory* isn't found in its two-dimensional graphic but the ability to transform the Third Circle Theory into the Destiny Theory. If we look at all three circles at once, we see a separation from all three and can draw a line through all three circles, as we did earlier.

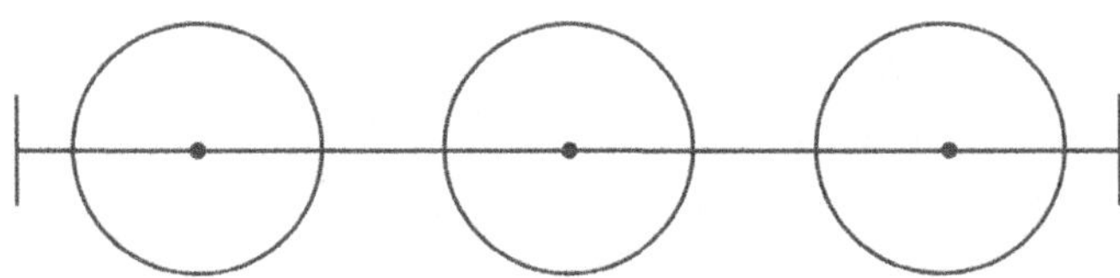

This signifies that we look at life as a flat timeline with a beginning and ending. However, the evolution of man through these three stages occurs from a state of expansion, not just forward progress. That means that we technically transpose all three circles on top of one another and realize that we are looking at the stages of evolution like a pyramid with each step (circle) to the top being smaller.

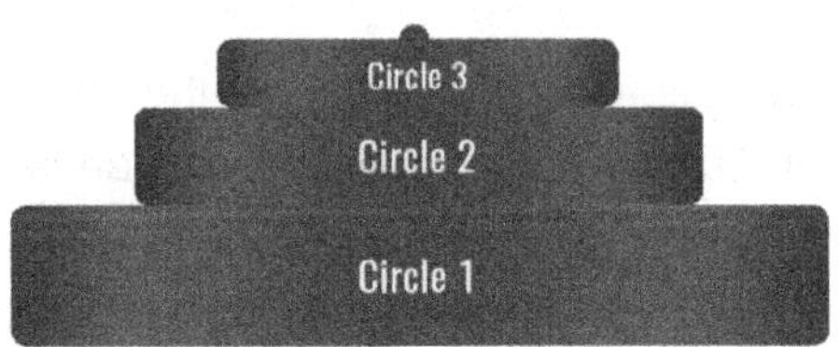

This signifies that, through this evolutionary path, man simply reaches his true SELF. In Circle 1, you noticed the SELF in the center; in Circle 2, you noticed the SELF in the center; and in Circle 3, you become the SELF.

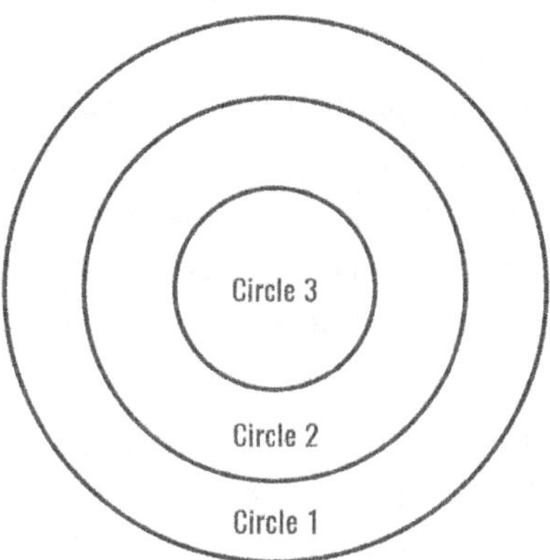

From this third-dimensional view, point you will realize that the SELF was and has always been the center point surrounded by EGO. As you evolve, you unveil the SELF by peeling off the EGO with each state of evolution you progress through.

The EGO becomes the prison when you reject the advancement of your psyche. The evolution of man requires overcoming masters, and pursuing the commitment to mastery in order to find its purpose and give birth to reputation.

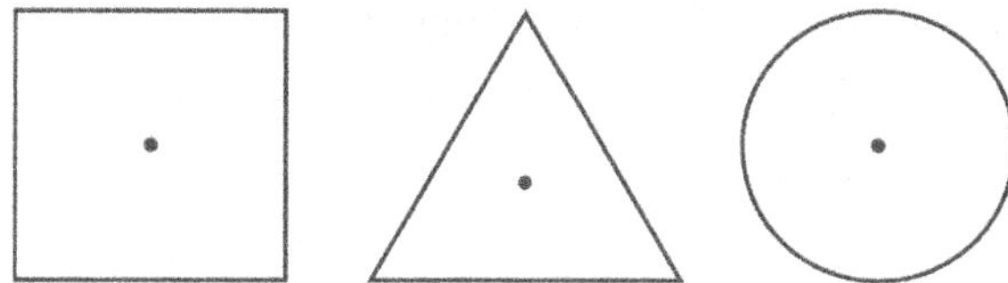

Most men understand the idea of being prisoners to others, enslaved to society and to the idea of money and conformity, but they often fail to realize how to progress from this stage on to the next. This state of stagnancy creates a strong state of EGO from a very early age, forcing man to accept his circumstance instead of overcoming it.

When man rejects society, he rejects the idea of overcoming its own shadow. He then becomes trapped in the comfort of his EGO, a place where conformity is greater than mastery. Since mastery requires time, it is often the misunderstanding of time that keeps man trapped in his EGO. It is because man seeks a way out of society, rather than seek to master it.

As a result, he finds himself back at the same place where he started with each attempt. Those who commit to mastery, however, find themselves in situations that enable them to use such mastery to overcome the experience of life faster, allowing them to focus on their purpose and reputation, rather than being stuck in their circumstance.

The concept of Destiny isn't one that requires giving up control of your direction or life. It also isn't based on man having a guaranteed path, but rather a chosen cosmic purpose. Having a cosmic purpose does not mean that an outcome has been pre-written, but rather an opportunity has been predetermined. Think of this as no different than knowing that winning the Olympics leads to glory, fame, and a gold medal, but nonetheless, still requires a good amount of work to do so.

Completing a full cosmic cycle will involve overcoming masters, committing to mastery through wisdom and, more importantly, accepting that while our destiny is preset, it isn't predetermined that we will get there.

Relationships: Shared Experiences

We discussed earlier the mental prison that man accepts early on during his journey of awakening. Part of that mental prison includes his perspectives on relationships, attempting to make things last forever.

As children, we want our friends to remain our friends forever. When we meet a romantic partner, we label them as "the one" at a very early stage, even if we don't yet truly know them. The same occurs with our attachment to a job or career, thinking this one will yet possibly be what we are meant to do in this world.

These attachment and dependency issues come from man's thought, which is a prison. This confinement is defined geometrically as a square, a structure with four hard edges identified with its sharp beginnings and endings. Man's psyche can be identified as a square in its pre-awakening stage; it can also be identified as having a need to attach to others in the same manner, expanding its state of imprisonment, rather than evolving. This is no different than accepting that getting promoted at a job you hate still leaves you working for the same company.

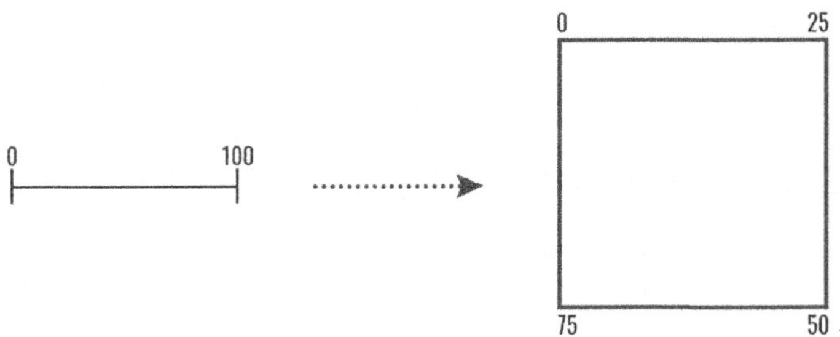

In this graphic, we take the SELF that man is at its unconscious stage (very surface level individual) and break down the 100-year timeline into a prison. We see that doing so provides man with four quadrants of his life: his imprisonment at each 25-year stage, totaling his 100-year lifeline. There is an important aspect of symbolism here in a square. It is the clarity that an unconscious life is one that builds relationships that are based on EGO, not the SELF. We see here that the connections we make with each and every other person are only geared to exist and connect to on a surface level during only one quadrant of our life.

People who live in a state of mental imprisonment don't evolve. They find a way to **justify their lack of capacity for evolution by seeking comfort in others who suffer from the same fate.**

This is how Herds are formed: common, imprisoned thinking not in search of wisdom, but rather in search of validation.

Such bonds are strong as long as both parties remain attached to the same core ideals and value systems. They will eventually shatter as time progresses, despite the fact that man himself may not evolve. Each stage of life brings a new value system, regardless of whether or not there is a progression from awareness to consciousness.

Let's look at "why" by transposing the Third Circle Theory principle over the first square of the Gate of Choice.

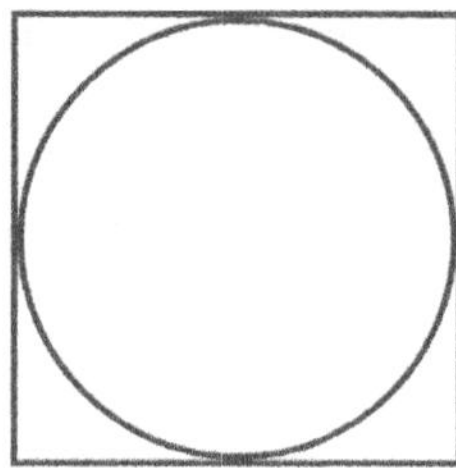

What we get is a circle (Psyche) trapped in a square (Prison of Circumstance), which shows us that the mind is forced to adapt and grow as a prisoner, rather than freely. This means that man stays stuck in the prison of the First Circle, which means that while time progresses, the psyche does not. As a result, it gives birth to the stages found in the First Circle, remaining a prisoner of it, rather than evolving to the second. This lack of progression of energy creates the various cycles known as the Birth Stage, the Settler Stage, and the Dreamer Stage.

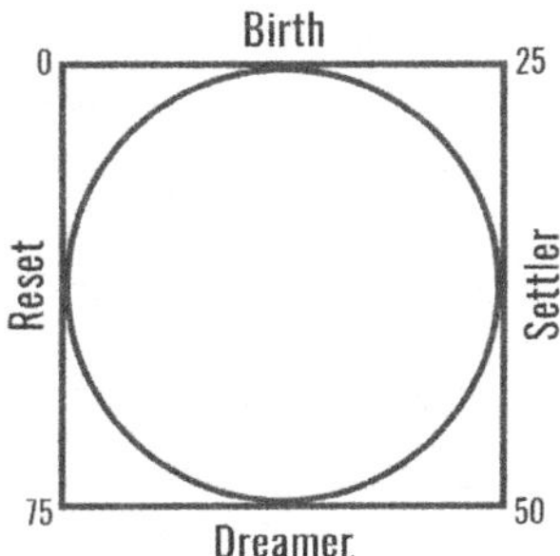

With each new stage that man enters imprisoned, he forms relationships of the same level. Children play together, the Settlers find one another, and the Dreamers surround themselves with more Dreamers. Since evolution isn't the goal of those in these stages, they simply form relationships that expand their EGO, rather than challenge their psyche.

Their expectations of relationships are drowned in the fears that they will lose them, rather the focus of experiencing them. While neither they nor the relationships evolve, time becomes the driver of the separation. ***Time does what man isn't willing to face***. Unbeneficial relationships formed on EGO eventually fall apart as each person evolves to a new phase; the other no longer identifies a sense of safety from being around that person.

The earlier stages of life can seem scary and those afraid to face it attach to others for fear of going through it alone. Think of that the same as you think about why those people with no skills partner together in hopes of starting a business. Most would pick their partners based on their strengths, but people stuck in this stage often pick their partners based on a void of skill and simply leverage that as an opportunity to not undertake the journey alone—not from a place of growth but rather fear.

In this graphic, you can see each relationship can only attach to one quadrant of life. As a result, you experience longer expectations of relationships, based on the length of each cycle's prison sentence. Relationships that are free and evolutionary are never made by those trapped in this stage.

As man evolves in society and removes the boundaries of his thought, he moves into comes the Second Circle, overcoming society, defined earlier as the Creation Stage. This is the stage in which creation and aspiration lead the way to transformation. We can geometrically draw this by once more defining the psyche (a circle), but this time being trapped in a transformation stage (shown here as a triangle).

The interesting observation here in this particular stage is how much closer the triangle's hard lines are to the circle itself. This is the stage where the EGO and the SELF start to blend, in hopes that the SELF evolves rather than falls victim to man's shadows. In this stage of life, the connection is formed around dependency rather than growth. It is more adaptive in nature than the First Circle since those in this stage can adapt to others in various stages of their own life.

Being stuck in the Second Circle and undertaking the three stages—known as the Awakening, Leader, and Achiever—is much better than being held in the First Circle. This progression means one is already accepting to learn societal concepts. In addition, relationships in the Second Circle are not linear but adaptive to both the First and Second Circle people. When the mind becomes adaptive, relationships follow suit.

With the larger scope of experiences found in societal acceptance comes the larger number of relationships in general the expectation is and remains "dependency" as the connection, while being adaptive, is still non-evolutionary. The ultimate prison guard "time" becomes the only driver for the advancement from one to the next.

In this graphic, such relationships are illustrated as being flat surfaces creating support for one another but also adaptive enough to connect with individuals stuck in squares from the First Circle. During an attempt at mastering society, the scope of relationships comes from the capacity of unleashing creativity and requiring unity around or during the Leader phase, which could create relationships with employees who are not always self-selected by ourselves but rather often united around the creativity of our work.

If man finds himself focused on his evolution, he will find himself in the Third Circle. Here, the SELF consumes the EGO. As a result, man views relationships in a different way, no longer in the sense of dependency, but as an opportunity for shared experiences. The lifecycle changes and is no longer trapped, as illustrated here.

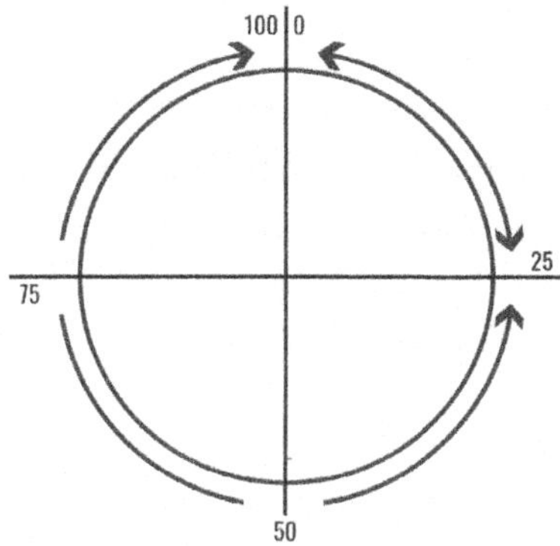

Each quadrant within the circle represents the physical time, not the experience of it. There is no longer a boundary of separation of cycle, as in the previous two cases. The vision, the purpose and rebirth of the Third Circle are now no longer attached to a separation of physical time but experienced through *all* of time. When the EGO is consumed by the SELF, the physicality of time no longer remains a prison, as man is no longer afraid of losing time, but simply experiences life. The relationships formed during such a state of consciousness are no longer defined by the prison of quadrants of physical time but approached through unlimited experiences focused on progression.

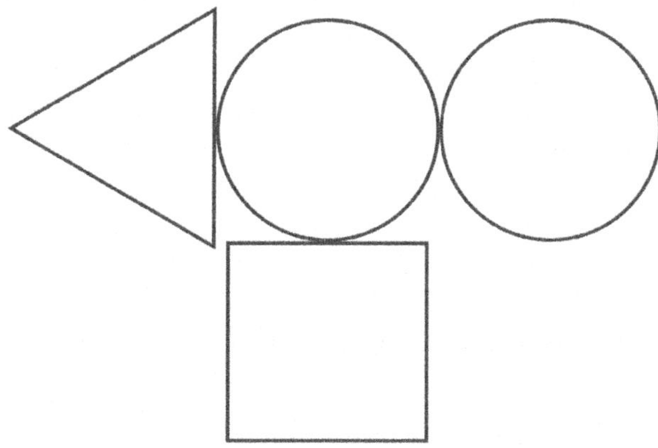

In this graphic, notice that regardless of whom the relationships are formed with, the circle never attaches surface for surface to the square or triangle the way they would with each other, it simply shares an experience, making it never dependent on the other. *This can also be showcased in day-to-day life by those not attached to their job or money, but rather their trade, craft, or mastery. They are not attached to marriage or commitment to someone but rather the ability to love. And they are not attached to those who fill a void, but rather freed through relationships with those who help create.*

The idea is to understand that **man's relationships are not forged by their endurance of time, but rather by their common opportunity of experiencing time together**. Too often, we dwell on keeping certain people around, expecting others to lead us. We fail to that as we evolve as humans, so do the relationships we undertake and, more importantly, our expectations and experiences of them.

It is key to our evolution to understand the meaning of the relationships we form and that each and every person we bring into our circle to share an experience leaves an imprint on our personality. These people can have great or devastating effects on our own evolution. From friends who prevent us from growing because of their fears of losing us and thieves who rob us of our time through deceit to those who aspire and inspire us to live a life in search of further wisdom, we all share one ecosystem. It is, however, up to us to carefully choose those whom we wish to share experiences with, in hopes of forging a personality closer to the SELF than lost in its EGO.

Earth: The Ecosystem of Personality

I once cried out for God's help and I was shown an opportunity, I once asked God for help and nothing happened.

This is the basis of man's constant struggle to buy into the existence of a Supreme Being—as so many suffer, so many need help, and so many cannot seem to validate the purpose of their existence on Earth. We earlier

examined the existence of the snail in our dimension and its relativity to the single dimension it occupies. We broke down the interaction and differences in speed between the snail in its one-dimensional existence and third-dimensional man.

While our existence occurs within two, distinctly separate, dimensional fields, it still occurs here on Earth and in the same ecosystem. We can coexist with snails, despite our variances of speed, and can experience time differently yet in the same space together. While the snail exists in our ecosystem and man does care for preserving such elements in his ecosystem, man cannot spend his life caring and paying attention to all elements and occurrences in such a vast ecosystem. This reality is why the ecosystem's existence is also irrelevant to man's timeline, but represents an environment used to foster the mind and experience of man on his individual timeline.

Simplifying this relationship means that the Earth continues to exist, regardless of each individual life that physically exists here. The same can be said for the ecosystems around us. Nature plays its own role, as new life is born and dies every second. Many of us have a lifecycle happening right in our back yards, inhabited with trees, plants, animals, and insects living and dying around us. Yet, we are often unaware of this life. Even if you cared to preserve your back yard to protect this ecosystem, you still wouldn't be able to account for every worm, every insect, and every snail living within your boundaries. You wouldn't be able to intervene with every conflict that arouses on a dimensional field.

In addition to the lack of awareness man has of such dimensions running their course, each dimension holds its own language, making it impossible to communicate through fields with the simplicity of one language.

In short, while you may be able to find ways to communicate with your cat, dog, tiger, zebra or snail, you have no definitive way to teach them language. In its place, you associate words with actions. Any form of communication or language regardless that it is a roar or a purr has only meaning to others who operate on a similar playing field, none above or below such wave-lengths.

If snails are one element of our ecosystem, then we can use the same string theory we discussed earlier to understand that we ourselves are part of someone else's ecosystem. While we may scream, moan or beg for help from others outside of our realm of vision and understanding—such as a God-like figure—they may not always be in a position to hear or understand us, especially if we use language as our primary form of communication.

Secular language works in a manner of identifying and communicating patterns infused in our brain to understand each other within the constraints of society; however, it is not the universal language. Energy and symbols (much like the Gate of Choice and Third Circle Theory's circle, triangle, square, and how they're arranged) hold definitions, codes, meanings, and instructions that are interpreted differently based on the level of consciousness. Some of these messages and use of language have been around since the dawn of time. They have not been hidden in any sense but meant for those with the capacity to understand and receive them to interpret.

For example, if a green crane symbol is drawn in the sand, a snail may crawl through it, experiencing this symbol. It does not in any capacity of consciousness decipher the connecting link between language of dimensions. If a two-dimensional being, like a dog, sees the symbol, it may dig and/or sniff it. A third-dimensional being may see the symbol and think that it means that something like a crane, or that a crane is a bird and so someone is trying to communicate a message about this specific bird in a vast array of context. A fourth-dimensional being may interpret the symbol not only as when (time) it was scripted in that exact location (space), but also a greater connection to consciousness as to what the crane repre-sents. In itself, the fourth-dimensional being interprets the crane as life and that the green color may not simply mean someone wanted to show a green crane but that the modality of life, flight, and growth (green) all are symbolic of the faculty of nature's creation and progress. The same symbol and vibrations can be interpreted differently, even though universally experienced across dimensions. This is no different than our inability to be conscious of the ecosystems we control —especially if the ecosystem we believe we inhabit isn't just the Earth but the galaxy or galaxies in which the Earth exists.

The question that now still remains unanswered is **what is the purpose of the ecosystem if not to prepare us for something?**

If you put a box in your living room and placed inside of it a few rocks and a few leaves and you inserted snails to observe them for the next six months, you might realize that some will try to escape the box and others will live in the confines of the four walls.

In other words, you have created a simple ecosystem, one that some snails will appreciate and honor, and some, feeling trapped will want to escape from. This experiment can be adapted to a similar idea that the Earth could present a similar experiment for us to learn to escape from, evolve past, or even learn to exist in. No different than controlled experi-ments we create for our own ecosystem, other higher-dimensional beings could create theoretically similar experiences for us.

The ecosystem we exist in helps us experience and overcome the 48 karmic lessons left as challenges on Earth—48 core lessons that will bring forth one ultimate personality worth carrying to the next realm, a choice of what we become in the next realm and the opportunity to leave behind an imprint of such choice as our reputation in this ecosystem.

This process allows those who seek a similar transformation and choice the opportunity to unite around our creation. Successfully overcoming each karmic path gives man access to a hidden bridge. The bridge that connects this third-dimensional ecosystem to the gate of the fourth, known as the Gate of Choice.

PART I: The Bridge

"Nobody can build the bridge for you to walk across the river of life, no one but you yourself alone. There are, to be sure, countless paths and bridges and demi-gods which would carry you across its river, but only at the cost of yourself; you would pawn yourself and lose." —Nietzsche

In this section, we will analyze the bridge that connects the third and fourth dimensions, leading to the Gate of Choice. We will analyze the journey that we must undertake, starting with leaving our societal beliefs to arriving in front of the Gate of Choice. We will also analyze some of the definitions we must pay attention to in order to ensure that we have shed our EGO, do not fall victim to our shadows on the way, and are ready to face a reflection of each and every karmic path lived. This final journey must be taken alone, in hopes that by the final step, we will have accepted the forged personality we see in our reflection, and that we will be ready to face our choices.

Societal evolution: One's ability to seek higher meaning

"When the whole world is running towards a cliff, he who is running the opposite direction seems to have lost his mind" —C.S Lewis

It is hard to ignore that it becomes harder and harder to escape society's grasp on our values as the population increases and more and more humans become prisoners than pioneers. **We live in a world of envy, a world where our own fellow humans would prefer to watch us fail, rather than succeed**—partially because of their own incapacity to escape from their very own prison. *A prisoner would, of course, be jealous of a free man. Yet even in the scope of free will, it seems that prisoners would* *prefer to watch the free man fail in his attempt to escape, rather than escape their very own prison.*

Going against everything we have been taught is a difficult task that man hasn't always been ready for. It requires courage, belief, a commitment to mastery and excellence, and the ability to face one's self. The journey to freedom isn't paved in glory but in man's ability to overcome his own deceit, his own judgment, and his own EGO.

At some point on the journey of evolution, man must learn to become his own Hero and undertake the journey necessary not to abandon or leave society but to overcome its boundary of control. He must relinquish his fears of the repercussions of disobedience and instead focus on giving a higher meaning to his life, one that can establish a reputation on his ecosystem rather than in society. This is the power of separating society from life and understanding that our impact in one echoes in the other while not automatically making us victors.

Societal evolution is defined by one's courage to leave, rather than escape. It is the opportunity to seek higher meaning and undertake a difficult journey, despite being given all the tools and capacity to stay comfortable as a master of others. Remember the importance and power of overcoming our mental prisons and becoming masters of our crafts, rather than being bound to masters.

Once man has become a master by completely overcoming the Second Circle and enters the Third, a critical choice remains. In *Third Circle Theory,* we learned that we face a choice to manipulate or impact. We encounter the choice to retain the comfort earned or to embark yet on another journey of evolution, a journey where we leave the comfort behind for the wisdom ahead. This new journey requires us to relearn and remaster ourselves, especially since the journey is no longer crafted in our understanding of societal control, but rather in the opportunity of shedding the same EGO we learned to build to make sense of the bizarre world we live in. While it may seem like yet another phase of life, this journey is actually quite different, a quest with an opportunity for transformation, or should I say, "evolution."

Quest: A Lifetime Journey in Search of Wisdom

The more consciousness a man unveils within himself, the more he seeks to make sense of his existence. Man's sole purpose without consciousness is to identify a reason for his being on Earth. Man's sole purpose with consciousness is to validate such purpose, and more importantly, use it to cross over from his third-dimensional state to his fourth. For such a large answer to manifest itself, man must look deeper in himself to ensure he is willing to undertake such a journey, as a journey can turn into a never-ending quest if he is not ready for the answers he may find along the way.

We spoke earlier of the biggest questions that man has tried to answer, starting with the relevancy of our existence here on Earth and continuing to the existence of God. These questions often are asked from those who need the answers the least, as they do not seek the validation of their SELF, but rather for the fear of disobedience. Those with a higher level of consciousness often do not need such answers, and as a result, do not partake in seeking compliance to a set of rules or guidelines they must abide by. Instead, they rather focus on finding what I call a "universal truth", one that bridges their third-dimensional purpose with the idea of what comes next. It is this very same bridge that becomes the core focus of their lifelong quest. Its relevance is more geared towards testing the psyche and its alignment to the vessel, and to decipher the intent of the personality that occupies it.

Crossing such a bridge from a third-dimensional SELF to a fourth requires shedding the EGO, forging of personality and the strength to face all your shadows. Shadows and EGO are life lessons one must learn to overcome and should not simply ignore. They are, in the end, no different than man's opportunity to show his choice of wisdom over deceit and to have adopted his commitment to seeking such universal truth. In other words, man must learn to cross the bridge by having faith in himself and his self-created value system rather than a value system created by his previous masters.

One can describe such a quest as an awakening, an opportunity to face one's shadow. Man is awakened and shown a universal truth, one that is far from convenient, one that has been hidden for years from masters in hopes that fear would not paralyze those who are enslaved. Call it a matrix, a world where a veil has been placed over the eyes of those who live in such a state of being. When man makes a decision to remove that veil from his eyes and face himself, he travels across this bridge, evolving past his society value system. The bridge that connects his perceived and conditioned truth to a universal one is not bound by the limitation of his vessel and third-dimensional SELF.

Choosing to embark on this quest is accompanied by the danger of man losing his identity as a whole. He would have to shed the identity that society has established for him and could face the possibility of never finding the identity of the SELF.

Imagine a journey where you transition from a beautiful fairy tale, one filled with opportunity, equality, beauty, and peace. From here, you are thrown into a place filled with war, destruction, isolation, and insecurity—a place so dark that only the wisdom you have accumulated can guide you back to the light you seek. As you enter this new world, you walk into it with hope, strength, and the need to discover the truth, but the time it takes you to face yourself takes its toll on you.

It becomes a never-ending quest with no direction, no roadmap, no guarantee that you are even heading in the right direction. You start to experience the world for what it is, not what you were taught to believe it is. The more your eyes open to this new universal truth, the more your shadows (societal veil) remind you that you made the wrong choice and that your masters were trying to protect you from experiencing such pain. Doubt, fear, regret, and panic hit you at once, in hopes of turning you back and no longer seeking truth but rather comfort and safety.

Those who endure this pain, this shift, this awakening, are rewarded with the opportunity to be free from the bounds of their masters. In return, they are given an opportunity to bind to their capacity for creativity; they can paint their environment and those in it to any shape or color they see fit.

Those who fall victim to their EGO and their need for comfort find themselves turning back and accepting the worship for their masters once more. They once trade their capacity for evolution to the fourth dimension for the comfort of their existence in the third.

Few will make it through this bridge, most will fail, and some will forever be trapped on the bridge, too far from its beginning and too far from its end, paralyzed by the fear of going forward and experiencing more, and petrified of going back for fear of failing. These people will remain stuck between these two realms, in need of guidance from masters who no longer exist in this realm and a gate at the edge of the bridge that will not open to the EGO that has yet to be overcome.

Imagine in the simplest of act, one's choice to pursue their creative talents through entrepreneurship as an example of such journey.

Imagine a person who has been fired from their job and rejected by society. This individual has been reminded by their masters of their lack of worth. Next, this person chooses to believe in them self enough to get started. They do so with excitement, with belief, and with the encouragement of others. They expect this change in their choice to lead them to fame, fortune, and freedom, but years go by and their resources are depleted. Their support mechanisms disappear, their self-belief shrinks, and they are reminded of the fun, security, and simplicity they held before making the leap. They forget the betrayal of their masters and now resort to justifying the search for a new master in order to ease the pain.

The majority of people in this jobless situation will go back and give control of their lives back to their masters, few will move forward with the correct energy, despite the pain and gain. They earn their freedom of time while the remaining few who have witnessed both sides of the coin will remain wedged between not working with enough velocity to gain their freedom and just enough to not go back to being enslaved. They will therefore forfeit this need to evolve and instead justify their failure by allowing their EGO to protect them from having to face it. They will support failure by making themselves believe that their humility and gratitude is what truly grants them freedom, creating once more held in a new mental prison, rejecting their path to evolution for their need for comfort.

When man makes a choice to face his shadow and embarks on the final journey of his third-dimensional evolution, the journey of acquiring consciousness and forging a final personality, man will be exposed to certain inexplicable events, events that cannot be described rationally in the third dimension. Such acts are often associated by those who have yet to master themselves as "help from the other side" or "God" being their guide. It is in times of desperation and fear in this journey that man often seeks a new master, when in reality, it is the beginning of man's exposure to the art of manifestation.

Values: The Manifestation of Higher Ideals

The strong individual loves the Earth so much, he lusts for recurrence. He can smile in the face of the most terrible thought: meaningless, aimless existence recurring eternally. The second characteristic of such a man is that he has the strength to recognize—and to live with the recognition—that the world is valueless in itself and that all values are human ones. He creates himself by fashioning his own values; he has the pride to live by the values he wills." —Frederick Nietzsche

Facing your greatest SELF comes from the ability to know that your potential has not been limited by other individuals' value systems. While the majority of the Herd is paralyzed by their EGO and their inability to choose between comfort and aspiration, those who are guided by the SELF have, through their life, created a sense of self-dependency, not so based on control mechanisms but rather on aspiration and creativity. Value systems driven by creativity and aspirations are often evolutionary in nature as they force man not to see himself as a result of what he has been thought or given, but rather by the experiences that have shaped his life.

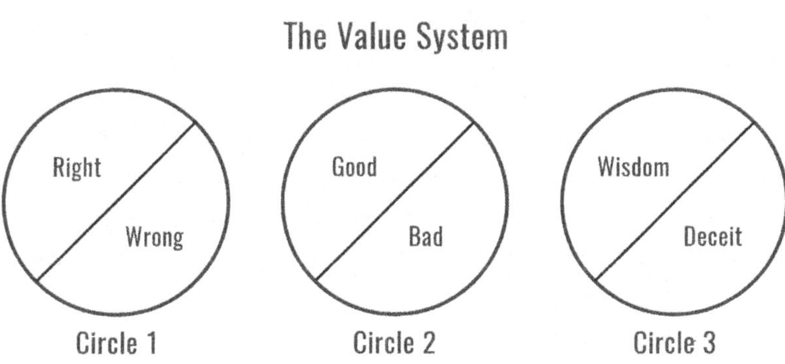

We discussed earlier the power of experience: If we believe that time and space are one, that through the experiences of life, one forges a personality driven by his reputation. Reputation is the byproduct of unity around creation (entrepreneurship). It is also our value system that enables us to advance to our evolution at an even faster pace than before. A value system driven by imagination and creativity is not hindered by other individuals' capacity or lack of belief.

Man, in his spiritual infancy often derives his belief system (values) from what he has observed, seen, or experienced. He consecutively lowers his aspiration to mirror or match that of those who have previously walked in his place. We can see examples of value systems created from imagination by observing the likes of Elon Musk, who did not limit his belief to what others have previously done, but rather around what's possible from his perspective. Musk's past experiences pushed his value system to allow the belief that colonizing another planet is a possibility, even though no one has previously done so. *This level of aspiration leads men like Elon Musk to create a new value-based system not rooted in previously limited thoughts but rather one that encompasses what is needed to create what is possible.*

A new value system requires the willingness to defy the masses, as the majority of man still remains imprisoned and incapable of seeing past what others have accomplished. This is the basis for why so many seek mentorship from those who have acquired what they desire. The mentee views the mentor's accomplishments as the benchmark of the top of their beliefs. By doing so, the mentees are appeasing their EGO, rather than attempting to discover the SELF. The SELF isn't a byproduct of the copy of someone else's belief, but the creation of a new belief system, one built with your own evolutionary journey in mind.

With the quest for a higher value system comes the capacity for higher ideals. Creativity above that which has already been created, excellence that allows such creativity to manifest to life in a manner that has yet to be experienced. A higher value system opens man to the idea of judgment, not based on conformity but on evolution.

Judgment: Creation of Your Own Values

One of the most clever ways the religious establishments have been able to turn religion from a state of evolution to a state of control has been focus on the final judgment. They embed the idea that, once a life is lived, it will be reviewed for its good and bad deeds. As a result, judgment will be placed on man whose faith will be decided by God, based on man's ability to have lived through his words. The idea of belief in a Higher Power or faith doesn't deter man from reaching a higher level of consciousness, unless it becomes worship rather than belief. However, this belief does force a level of obedience if man chooses to accept that his judgment is driven not by his choices but by his commitment to worship.

As discussed in *Third Circle Theory*, faith changes as man evolves from a level of awareness to a state of consciousness—the progression of connecting church to broader his range of thought becomes (as it should in an evolutionary state, rather than an institutionalized one). The more consciousness in man, the less fear is diverted from control mechanisms. This is no different than the observation of "the richer the man, the less fear of societal law occurs". Freedom to evolve from control is driven by the freedom of the judgment that comes from disobedience.

If you do not fear the ticket, you will speed.

If you do not fear getting arrested, you will live as you please, even if morally wrong by societal standards.

It can be said that if man weren't afraid of the judgment of God for his "bad" deeds, his value system would certainly differ. The issues of control arise from breaking down good versus bad as good judgment metrics. We then become prisoners of the societal standards of living, both in fear and restrained from pushing for our highest aspirations.

In order for man to face his true SELF as he travels on the final bridge to the Gate of Choice, he must have the capacity to recognize the personality that has been forged. For that reason, man must be willing to decipher his choice in living, based either on his own self-created set of values or by the values provided for him, those that keep him restrained and confined.

Did man follow his highest aspirations or was man limited to the safety of his comfort?

While judgment—also known as choice—does occur in allowing man to face an open-versus-closed gate, it is more aligned with the idea of having lived through the Destiny Theory and having learned the power to overcome one's SELF rather than to have obeyed the idea of institution. **The final choice will ultimately be a review of man's choice rather than his obedience.**

Did the choices that man made during his third-dimensional life in his quest for personality allowed the development of his greatest version of himself?

In his quest to overcome and in deciphering man's capacity for true judgment based on the SELF and not the EGO, we look back at man's capacity for choice as it pertains to his choice of seeking wisdom versus deceit. Herein lies the question of how one deciphers between wisdom and deceit.

From one perspective, it is quite easy to tell them apart by looking at what arises from a lie, versus what arises from opportunity. In many cases, judgment is based on a previously accepted set of values. Such values could be clouded, formed from deceit. It would then be nearly impossible to know what life has deciphered as right and wrong, especially since we cannot even make sense of what society has deemed to be right or wrong, based on vague laws.

You can think of this as having free speech in the United States (as the law states). You should still be careful as to what you say; e.g., hateful comments may make you feel like you do not belong. The law creates a false sense of protection from prosecution, and it doesn't prevent judgment from others in the same societal realm.

One way to allow you to adopt a new set of values and pioneer a life driven by the SELF rather than the EGO is to create a simpler understanding of decision-making by breaking decisions into two categories:

Decision made for your personal gain versus decisions made for the common good of the race you represent.

Before breaking down definitions, allow me to clarify that decisions made for the common good are to be differentiated from one's choice of helping others. They are two very different things.

Decisions made for the common good represent man's ability to respect his ecosystem. These decisions enable him to receive wisdom, even if, at times, the decision doesn't lead to what seems to be a favorable outcome at first sight. One can choose to extort others in deceit in order to get richer. However, one isn't rewarded with wisdom (the universal currency); he simply gains short-term riches (societal currency). This person often faces a series of further deceptive choices that may lead him to state of imprisonment (both internally and physically). In choices made for the common good of the ecosystem, man is rewarded with further wisdom that enables his opportunity to make clearer choices in the future.

This is no different than saying that a choice is a fork in the road. While the chosen direction may be paved with difficulty—despite the intention of not being deceitful— the wisdom earned enables man to be prepared for the further obstacles ahead as man's role was never meant to be interpreted as easy but rather as an opportunity to overcome. What better way to overcome than to be met with choices that enable us to rise to our highest aspirations? A fork in the road, in the end, is just a piece of the journey and certainly not man's destination. Yet, it can be concluded that the more man chooses to deceive himself and others, the farther from his evolutionary destiny he will find himself.

Do not forget that, with such choices, man is forever challenged with the opportunity to self-reflect. He also faces an opportunity to create his own value system—not absorb one provided by society but establish one provided by his experience, thus overcoming himself and shedding his EGO. This value system will be the basis for earning his forged personality and will be tested as he crosses the bridge to face the Gate. With each new experience comes a higher level of consciousness, one that gives birth to a higher wavelength and awakens the power of the alchemist within.

Manifestation: Birth of Alchemy

Mystical in some books, magic in others, **the art of manifestation is the expansion of the SELF past the EGO.** When the SELF evolves past the EGO, an energy is created that enables itself to take better control of its own energy source, no longer separating the psyche from the vessel. As we discussed earlier with chakras, when the flow of energy is not blocked, many of these energy sources work together to transmit data and create and energy source beyond our third-dimensional selves. In many cases, our inability to control such force is what draws the energy out to a state when only its opposite force can stop it.

In other words, the energy expands until it meets a force that stops it. Think of your heart as an energy source. In its purest form, the attracts those who also have pure hearts. I am sure you have heard that you get from the universe what you put out. If you seek to deceive, deceit finds you. If you seek to learn, wisdom finds you.

The art of manifestation is your ability to expand and contract your consciousness.

Manifestation seems to be uncontrollable at first, as most people don't realize what they manifest until it has shown up. It is often part of the learning that occurs on the bridge on your way to the Gate as your consciousness develops. You reach a state where you have grown the SELF past the EGO. This lack of control is an opportunity to switch one's method of communication from language that is linear from beginning to end (like an alphabet), to language that is continuous and never-ending like a circular clock. The switch forces you to learn to communicate with energy, not with words.

Man has always believed language to be an important form of communication, but never looked at language as a continuous form, one not bound by the need for a beginning and end. Language is a constant vibration, one that gives meaning to man's existence and his identity, not to the space he occupies. This is a pivotal part of the journey for man to shed his boundary and reshape his understanding of time, as time is always the master from which no third-dimensional being can free himself. Time is also the boundary that divides these two dimensions.

When man forfeits his need to look at language from beginning to end, he forfeits his need to communicate through his third-dimensional vessel. Instead, man learns to communicate through his psyche. This is the reason some people can simply look into your eyes and know just about everything about you or why music sparks incredible feelings of joy, sadness, or aspirations in people. Music isn't impactful for its lyrics, but the feelings that the beats create.

As much as man can expand energy into the universe, he can also receive energy from other beings in the universe who have expanded their energy in an attempt to communicate. **A man with a purpose expands so much energy that it attracts other energies that seek a similar purpose.** This is often the reason we cross paths with others who have common beliefs and value systems. During that expansion, we seem to find allies who are not around us in their physical form but can be felt through our energy.

The better we get at communicating without boundaries, the more we realize that these vibrations we feel have always been there. We were not in a position to listen, as we were seeking to hear with our ears and speak with our mouths rather than feel through our vessel. As a result, we missed the access we have always had to the hidden knowledge that exists in such vibration—knowledge not geared to learn, but that opens a door to our own evolution.

It is this knowledge that we have forever labeled as "alchemy."

Alchemy: A Bridge to Hidden Knowledge

Some call it magic. Others, witchcraft. Some believe it to be divine, but what if alchemy was man's ability to channel communications from those living in the fourth dimension?

Many inventors, including Isaac Newton, kept journals of their alchemy practices that were discovered years after their passing. In his journals, Newton actually gave credit to this art for many of his discoveries, including his theory on gravity. He claimed that he channeled information pertaining to his discovery during his search of the philosopher stone, a stone in alchemy that represents man's ability to have discovered the highest level of consciousness. Many have claimed the stone to be a real physical item, others believe it to be a metaphor of man's evolution. What if Newton's gravity theory or any of his discoveries weren't his to begin with, but instead were given to him during his search of further wisdom on his very own bridge?

Alchemy has always been defined as one's ability to turn lead into gold, which basically symbolizes one's ability to commit to the mastery of taking something of no value and making it valuable. This is no different than entrepreneurship today, one's ability to use one's own excellence and mastery to bring advancement to the world or to the processes around it, turning creativity into value.

While alchemy sounds more magical and spiritual, its underlying definition is no different than entrepreneurship in the modern world, and no longer defined as witchcraft. Entrepreneurship isn't the modern-day replacement of alchemy, but rather the basis for preparing for alchemy—preparing to be in a position to undertake the information we receive once we reach such a high level of dimensional consciousness.

Alchemy is the tool that man is given once he has overcome his circumstance. He used it to regain his freedom from the masters who convinced him that his obedience was more important than his evolution. Man is rewarded for his commitment to wisdom by being given the opportunity to progress further through this very same hidden knowledge.

As described earlier, the chakras represent the opportunity for man to learn to channel energy and allow its flow to integrate the body and psyche together. But what if the integration of such energies could give birth to one's ability to not just channel energy but to open communications with the other side as well?

Most think of communication as language, which would mean that we would expect such communication to occur in the physical realm, but the art of alchemy doesn't occur in a third-dimensional state of being, but rather in a fourth. This would be similar to meditation in essence, but the focus would not be the basis of one finding his psyche—as it has already been connected to the vessel via the forged personality— but open communications with others in that fourth dimension.

Many who practiced alchemy in the past have attempted to connect their understanding and control of time to the process, in hopes of extending their own mortality. While many practiced this art in the hopes of creation or expansion into fields above and beyond the vessel itself, many also missed the idea that one becomes an alchemist because of his own evolutionary path rather than simply practicing alchemy.

You yourself have most likely undertaken some level of alchemy at some point in your life, and simply didn't realize it. You may have looked at it as a divine intervention, a gift from God, or the power of manifestation. In reality, the experience was the alchemist in you. Since all energy in the universe shares some level of connectivity, all people can channel the same energy, assuming, of course, they know how.

Think of the evolution of alchemy as a parallel to your own growth. In the graphic below, note the evolution of man's alchemy as it pertains to the internal evolution of man through his three stages of consciousness. The yin-yang symbol is used here to show the balance of dark and light as it also pertains to man's need for both light and shadow to practice alchemy, whether or not he is more or less conscious of it.

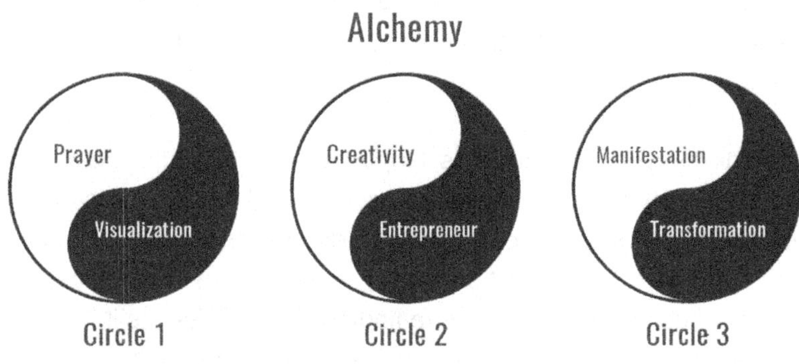

Circle 1: Prayer and visualization are very early stages of one expanding their energy in hopes of attracting "what they seek" in their life. While often seeking money or power, those in the First Circle indirectly long for growth and to be successful in their upcoming societal opportunities, which is why they are often the two most relevant requests during prayer and visualization. Those living in the First Circle haven't yet mastered circumstance. So, they seek their answers through their visual recognition of themselves or in the outside influences from which they believe their goals come to fruition.

Circle 2: Entrepreneurship and creativity represent a realm of consciousness in which man has shed his need to rely on God or external forces.

Instead, he develops his alchemy by learning to shift that focus into his creativity and then evolves it by undertaking entrepreneurship. Often geared towards a more physical approach to bringing to life a product or service, alchemy at this stage is still very much an art of turning a non-existent idea into a valuable commodity.

Circle 3: Manifestation and Transmission are the unity around creation that occurs in the Second Circle. Man understands his ability to create and unite, and as a result, seeks more of the same. He becomes faster and better at unity and creation, to the point where what he creates and who he chooses to unite change as his consciousness evolves. In this evolution, man starts to realize how to materialize all his thoughts from a fourth-dimensional vibration to a third-dimensional physical realm. It is in that process that his vibration becomes noticed by others who observe the evolution. In this moment, man is given a transmission to the location of a gate, as well as a task that enables him to manifest the key to this gate. Should man be capable of creating this key and uniting others around it, he will be able freely break the barriers that divide his existence in both realms. This is also often referred to as having chosen your purpose.

When man receives an opportunity to attain a key to opening the gate to hidden knowledge, he is given an opportunity to walk the final bridge that divides his existence between this realm and the fourth. On this bridge, man will face his greatest challenge yet: facing himself while committing to his chosen purpose.

The Bridge: A Test of Our Forged Personality

Every man steps off the platform of reproduction and is thrown into prisons from which they must escape—a prison of time, a prison of fear, a prison of EGO. These prisons become the ultimate test of man's capacity to rely solely on excellence and mastery to evade such boundaries and find the wisdom necessary to forge a personality worthy of carrying onward.

Throughout "the bridge" section, we have analyzed the various definitions that surround the transformation that man undergoes as he chooses to take the bridge to further his evolutionary state. We have also identified the tools that need to be mastered for man to embark on the long journey to the Gate of Choice.

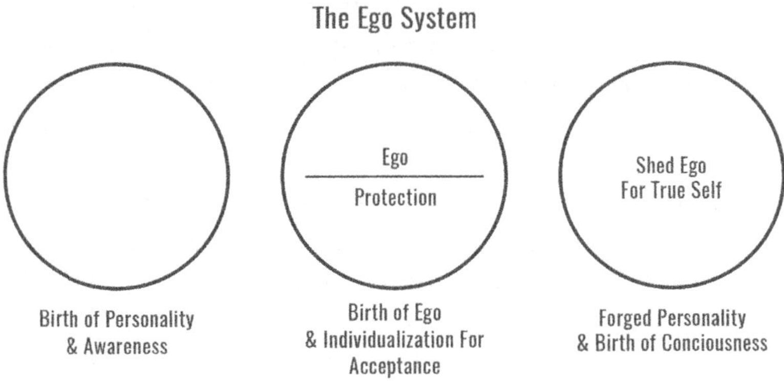

At the end of self-awareness and at the beginning of consciousness, the Higher Man will be given an opportunity to cross the bridge that leads to the Gate of Choice. This gate defines whether the evolutionary cycle took its place or it needs to reset in an attempt to start over.

It is up to man to have prepared his personality to no longer fear the unknown on the other side of time, the shadows that prevent the light, and EGO that reflect facing the SELF. It is only on this bridge that man will reflect if he has reached a level of wisdom worthy of carrying his forged personality onward.

During this journey of consciousness towards the Gate, man will have to reflect on one fundamental question in order to unlock the key to his evolution.

Did Man choose to pursue a life of Wisdom?

He then gains the ability to answer for his choices. Choices not defined by the right and wrong of society, not bound by the masters who have trained his perspective to accept deceit in exchange for comfort, but rather by the fundamental impact they have had on his reputation and wisdom.

During this journey on the bridge, man's personality is tested to ensure it is free of EGO, free of fear, and free of masters. This is the true test of man's identity in the universe, not just in a third-dimensional world. On each of the 48 steps (each representing a previously travelled karmic path) towards his destination, man will face a mirror reflection of himself. Whether in light or darkness, he will be challenged to answer for his deceit during each of his 48 karmic paths travelled. Should man have missed certain steps in his journey, his image of himself will change dramatically along the way and he will arrive at the Gate staring at a broken reflection of himself, one still a prisoner of his EGO, filled with a deceitful personality rather than a forged one.

He will have to go back and start the process all over. This bridge connects man's EGO to man's forged personality. The farther from the entrance of the bridge that man walks towards his gate, the more he loses his sense of physical self and the darker the path becomes, relying strictly on man's forged personality and belief in the SELF to guide the way. The more deceitful man has been to himself and others, the harder it will be for him to shed his EGO during this journey. As a result, he will lack the wisdom to navigate this bridge.

If man fails to have found the true SELF, if man fails to have forged a personality, and if man fails to have mastered his highest aspirations on this journey, then he will have fallen victim to his own deceit. Through his shadow and EGO, he will not find enough light to find the gate, let alone face it.

For his inability to act, man will have to once more find himself heading back to the roots of his comfort, to once more question his choice of wisdom over deceit and once more attempt to free himself from his EGO.

On the other hand, if man succeeds in his ability to answer for his choice of wisdom over his opportunity for deceit, and forges a personality worthy of the SELF, man will use his light to guide himself to the gate that waits at the end of this bridge. He will walk with firm belief of who he is, the reputation he has created, and more importantly, the wisdom he has accumulated. He will overcome himself one last time, free himself of any EGO, and find himself standing at the end of this bridge and in front of the Gate of Choice.

PART II: The Gate

"Judge me as I stand in front of the Gate, not for who I am today, but rather if I have become the man I was capable of becoming. Judge me for my choices toward wisdom and for my inability to overcome deceit. Judge me for choosing to overcome myself rather than give in to my shadow. Judge me for me, should I have overcome my EGO, or fail to judge me for my EGO has once more overcome me." —Pejman Ghadimi

Earlier, I explained the idea that only humans are bound to the prison of time and look at a clock as a baseline to create a beginning or end; whereas, astrology is a clock in its own right, a sense of beginning and ending but based on a dimension, not a vessel. A clock measures the ending of a vessel, an astrological sign, the forming of the personality that had to be mastered. This is how those who read astrology can tell you about the personality you are expected to form. It is their ability to link who you are based on a calendar to your destiny theory. This makes astrologers seem like they are able to see the future when, in reality, they are simply linking your existence to a dimensional clock, rather than a man-made one. Think of the zodiac as a 12-hour cycle, of a clock as a 12-hour cycle, and of the 48 personalities as quadrants of each of the four quadrants that make up a sign or hour of day (0, 15, 30, 45).

With each lifetime beginning and ending at the Gate comes an opportunity once more for the psyche to analyze its journey, form new contracts (more on this later), and reattempt or move on to the next personality. We've discussed the Destiny Theory and one's predetermined path, not pre-lived or pre-experienced, which means that it is possible that we ourselves are the ones choosing the overcoming, and more importantly, the opportunity or obstacles to overcome. This could be similar to choosing your avatar in a video game and the weapons it can access. While you haven't experienced the game, you could technically prepare for the upcoming challenges.

The Gate acts as a portal every time you overcome your personality. You are faced with an opportunity to undertake the bridge to the Gate each lifetime; you may be allowed to pass to the next personality to overcome based on your ability to shed the EGO and re-encounter the SELF, or you are sent back to again attempt to overcome. The Gate is your ability to accept the forging of your true personality, as it is a reflection of what you wished to overcome, versus what you became. Each one of the 48 steps has its own karmic gate that needs to be overcome in order to face the final Gate of Choice.

When man faces the Karmic Gate, he is stripped of his vessel in hopes of still being able to recognize himself in this time of passage, living through his psyche not his vessel. If man cannot do so in this moment, he will simply carry his EGO once more to find another vessel to occupy, in an attempt to give himself a personality worth carrying forward. If, however, man can overcome himself and master the personality cycle he was experiencing, he will be given passage to move forward past the gate and be given the next personality to overcome until all 48 are mastered.

Humanity: A Bridge to The Superman

“Man is something that shall be overcome. Man is a rope, tied between beast and overman—a rope over an abyss. What is great in man is that he is a bridge and not an end.” —Friedrich Wilhelm Nietzsche, *Thus Spoke Zarathustra*

We discussed the power of choice through a variety of definitions through the Gate of Choice, definitions meant to help you connect the capacity to live here with the capacity to overcome your SELF and evolve. You are, after all, the hero of your own journey. With each lifetime comes another opportunity to bridge your own evolution to once more return to the Gate.

Each bridge you cross successfully leads you one step closer to the final gate.

While man has to overcome himself with each lifetime, he must also overcome the Earth itself by graduating all timelines that encompass the final phase of his evolution, forging the personality not of man, but of the Superman.

Throughout this book, we've discussed the various evolutionary paths man encounters, from a state of imprisonment to a state of awakened consciousness. What we haven't yet covered is our ability to analyze the 48 forged personalities, the 48 karmic paths that allow man to become the Superman. Each personality forms one step that leads to becoming the Superman. Each personality forged in its own right isn't enough to become the Superman, but all personalities forged into one allow the birth of the Superman.

Before we dwell deeply into the idea of the Superman, let's analyze the 48 personalities man must master prior to evolving. Each karmic path is not related to an astrological sign, but rather a window of opportunity in a continuous time and space quadrant. Even astrology is, in essence, a map for fourth-dimensional beings, no different than time is to humans. It's interesting here to note that both time and astrology are referred to by the constraints of a circle, showing that there is no end to the zodiac as there is no end to time, without mentioning 12 hours per cycle, four quadrants per hour as 12 signs to the zodiac, four personalities per sign as we mentioned earlier. The point here is to mention that the graphic below is a mirror of a clock and that each zodiac sign (each lifetime here) is like one hour there. In each zodiac sign exists four quadrants as in each hour of our day.

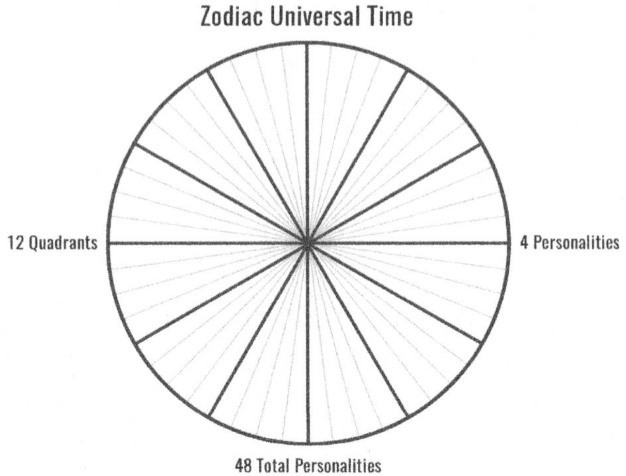

Once they have been overcome, these 48 karmic paths form the personality of the Superman. Regardless of the path you are on in this lifetime, you must have an overview of the entire bridge, not just one step. I have yet to prove if it is possible for man to overcome and master two karmic paths at once. I do believe that the more conscious man is of the journey he must face, the more capable he will be of recognizing how to properly overcome himself by preparing himself and his value system accordingly. I have found that the more exposed I was to these various paths and their core lessons, the more I realized who I was and where on the bridge I stood to face the final gate and my opportunity to overcome earth itself.

If you find yourself realizing that, for some unknown reason, you feel that you have already overcome a step because the path seems familiar to you in this lifetime, it is possible that you have. For this reason, the personality itself comes naturally to you. Remember that each forged personality is not forgotten with each passage through the gate. It is only forgotten in cases where the personality was fooled by the EGO, so a path was skipped or is being repeated. Each forged personality helps you retain the lesson learned throughout. While you may not remember the life you held or during which you overcame, you absolutely can feel naturally gifted with what you've already overcome in the one you are experiencing currently.

Since man writes his own destiny theory each and every time before he enters a new vessel to overcome all the experiences, man can choose based on his past karmic powers and all he has overcome how complex he wishes the destiny circle to be. That means that man could be faced with a self-imposed challenge to overcome more than one personality per vessel. The more complex the destiny circle, the more advanced the soul that undertakes it.

What matters is the importance beyond all other beliefs to overcome one's SELF, no matter the location, circumstance, or choice he faces.

The table of contents in this book should serve as a direction of the evolution, while the definitions themselves should allow you to refer to each throughout your journey in hopes of helping you connect the universal truth to each of the personalities you must overcome.

The reason none of these are in any particular order is because overcoming doesn't mean to not fail; it simply means to progress. While you may have attempted to forge personalities in the past, you may also have failed and skipped certain ones before having to revisit them through an alternative experience. It is important to understand each and every one of them in order to distinguish the Superman from man. Once one has mastered all 48 cycles, he is given the opportunity to be a guardian of time rather than a prisoner of it.

Since we are bound to time and cannot break free of its prison, it is our responsibility to overcome time so we may become masters of it.

Artistry: Establishing a value system

Discipline: Freeing of emotions and establishing discipline

Compassion: Learning the principle of the common good

Instruction: Learning to foster talent

Awareness: Finding awareness through beauty

Intention: Defining intent though focus

Introspection: Learning to unlock hidden chakras

Influence: Leading through influence, based on the SELF

Reform: Discovering how to put yourself second to purpose

Responsibility: Learn to be dependable

Inspiration: Aspirating to alchemy

Amplification: Creating unity around mastery

Expression: Linking alchemy to entrepreneurship

Consolidation: Accepting your identity

Articulation: Giving shape to your own value system

Mastery: Committing to mastery

Electricity: Cultivating internal energy

Freedom: Breaking free of society, committing to authenticity

Release: Managing your shadows

Consideration: Releasing the EGO from competition

Revelation: Shedding the EGO, and allowing creativity to lead the way

Extension: Devoting without expectation

Transcendence: Ridding societal limitations

Passion: Seeking the experience of time

Wonder: Remembering the innocence of the child

Individuation: Giving birth to self-awareness

Discovery: Allowing curiosity to expand the SELF

Empowerment: Validating the SELF through self-belief

Satisfaction: Separating the EGO from creation

Grace: Gaining a sense of finesse

Innocence: Learning to cultivate self-love

Modulation: Learning to compound knowledge

Liberation: Giving up right and wrong value systems

Translation: Communicating through energies

Experience: Experiencing time

Enchantment: Enchanting others with the SELF, not the EGO

Tenderness: Being gentle

Originality: Forging a final personality

Seduction: Learning manipulation for the greater good

Versatility: Understanding the power of intuition

Study: Learning the power of a commitment

Resolve: Persevering for your beliefs

Confidence: Leading oneself as well as others

Trust: Judging from the SELF, not the EGO

Structure: Becoming a master, advancing change

Solution: Seeking how to overcome

Grounding: Reaching your highest aspirations

All these personalities separately represent an opportunity to transcend the experience of time, and to be free of your humanity. Humanity is a rope tied between Beast and Overman (one who can overcome his own EGO), but one that can also lead to the Superman. Overcoming man isn't a task; it is the sole cosmic purpose of your existence in this third-dimensional realm and the basis for theological evolution.

To not overcome man means to reset and experience, to overcome means passage.

Hero: The Story of The Higher Man

To live as the Higher Man means to live a life of values not established by societal constraints, but rather by one's SELF, with the sole intention of evolution. One can choose to overcome judgment and the envy of others who cannot comprehend why such a value system would exist. It would, however, shatter their acceptance that we are all held to the same set of standards and are bound by the same societal law, rather than the universal laws that govern the energies they cannot experience.

To live as a Higher Man means to embrace the creativity and capacity of the connection that exists between the vessel and the SELF. One is then no longer imprisoned by the vessel but *becomes* the master of the vessel, learning not to shed the EGO but rather use it as a weapon. Armed with this mastery, he combats the distractions that can prevent the opportunity to forge a personality and imprint a reputation, almost like a shield that can protect the psyche from being harmed rather than preventing its experience.

To live as a Higher Man means to choose a life devoted to wisdom and evolution and to become the bridge that gives way to better men, men who are no longer conflicted by wisdom or deceit, men who choose the common good over their own EGO, and men who follow only because they wish to lead themselves.

To live as a Higher Man is to love higher, to love not for the fear of being alone but for the fear of not experiencing a connection. **Love is the language that connects all men, and an opportunity to share who you are, your gifts and reputation.** Love allows you to leave an imprint on others so that you help them no longer fear experiencing love, and don't hide their heart behind their EGO.

To live as the Higher Man means to overcome the thief that exists in all of us, to live a conscious and connected life, and to embrace the gift of impact. To realize the potential of the ecosystem placed here and to preserve it for others who can use it to progress, rather than destroy the ecosystem so it gives way to more thieves. The higher a man's aspiration, the deeper his roots for his capacity to do evil. To live as a higher man isn't to deny one's evil tendencies, but to choose to pursue a path of wisdom.

To live as a Higher Human means to have chosen a path and value system for wisdom, rather than one of deceit.

To live as a Higher Man means to be the hero of your journey, the one who creates the path, walks the path, and overcomes the shadows that are presented each and every time. It is so easy for man to fall victim to his deceit that real heroes are starting to lose their way to the Gate. This result occurs partly because of the overreaching effects of societal evolution putting a veil over humanity, and partly because overcoming requires rewriting your sets of values and beliefs. It is often in rewriting that man faces his darkest shadows.

In modern art, television, and movie-making, the hero is depicted as the one who sets out on a quest, who is met with obstacles and challenges and who, in his lowest point of failure, overcomes his life and finds meaning again to his journey, only to end it in glorious victory. But being a hero isn't always about a quest; it can also be a revolutionary way to evolve your consciousness.

Each and every journey we undertake requires us to become our own heroes, individuals whose heroic behavior isn't formed in theatrics or helping others but rather by the personality we form. It takes courage to defy the "status quo" and it takes courage to set your own sets of values as society will remind you countlessly of the consequences of your disobedience. It is in a unique internal value system that lies the ability to live life as a hero, one whose rules are set by the hero's own scale of judgment and not by the prison or fear of time.

When one can live their destiny theory as a Hero, one can walk through the completion of a lifecycle as closely aligned to one's path of SELF, not EGO. This is the ultimate way to overcome the experience of life and ensure passage through the karmic gate with the experience, skills, and personality intact.

Think of the 48 personalities as compounding; each time one is overcome, man retains the elements of the personality, going to the next phase stronger, more capable, and with higher intuition in an opportunity to once more overcome the next phase of challenges and opportunities while also carrying forward the proper cosmic and karmic energy. This is also referred to in many cases as "good karma."

A Closed Gate: A Life Lived as a Thief

"On my journey to forging my very own personality, I met two thieves: one who had accepted his fate and the other who simply stole because stealing was all he knew. I kept trying to help the thief who hadn't yet accepted his fate and realized only after I had failed to do so that I had turned into a thief myself, I had stolen my own time by attempting to help others, when I had yet to help myself." —Pejman Ghadimi

When man refuses to live as a Hero of his path and faces his challenges and overcoming with deceit, he retains his EGO. He is faced with the opportunity to overcome himself in the same setting as before but is also given further challenges, known as "debt with obstacles", which are much more difficult to overcome. In other words, he is not living in an evolutionary cycle but rather in one that forces him to face a harder circumstance in order to forge his personality. This debt can sometimes be so overwhelming that man no longer seeks to overcome but prefers to live life as a thief, living for survival and no longer evolving, at the cost of other souls.

One of man's most deceitful habits is his desire to help others. We are brought up to believe that we should help one another. We lend a hand

and step up when others call for help. We do so and gain a sense of false happiness disguised as "fulfillment", but yet we struggle to validate the feeling. We silently cry for help, hoping others will do for us what we have done for them, putting scales of values into debt and the power that comes from being owed.

More importantly, we rob ourselves of the opportunity to find wisdom by preventing others from falling victim to their own deceit. Being critical of the path to wisdom is simple for someone who has yet to walk it, someone who has yet to experience the suffering of transformation, and more importantly, someone who sends sheep to slaughter, only to prevent the experience of pain.

It has become so easy in modern society for men to give fellow men advice on how to succeed, how to love, whom to love, and what direction to take in life. Giving advice is the perfect remedy to not having to personally deal with the same scenario or issue. How often have you watched one person advise another how to live in perfect harmony in a relationship while they suffer from the very same issue and aren't yet capable of facing their own shadow in dealing with it?

The advice is spot on, helpful, and offered with good intent, but the experience is deflected onto the other party rather than the self. One tells another of a toxic relationship and how to escape it, yet fails to get rid of their own toxic relationships, due to the pain of the experience.

Day in and day out, man robs himself of the experience of life, knowing exactly what to do, yet fearing the pain or pleasure connected with the experience. The pain is too strong to bear and thy fear experiencing the pleasure, only to get a taste and never experience it again. A man who fears to live is a man robbing himself of the experience of life and, as a result, becomes his own worst enemy. That is the ultimate definition of deceit, to deceive one's self.

The evolution of the thief becomes a life lived in self-deceit, and also geared to rob others of the same experience. Regardless that the thief chose to steal or that he believes to have no other choice, **a thief** doesn't like to be labeled as such and so will hide in his own shadow. He **hopes to attract other individual's shadows in order to seduce them out of their light. This is the core of why misery loves company** and how man always finds others so easily when reflecting in his shortcoming, fear, or suffering, since most of mankind has yet to overcome the stage of suffering.

One can see this happen in the third dimension for the vessel and in society. In times of crisis, countries unite and people put away their differences. In times of growth and pleasure, man becomes selfish and allows the EGO to manipulate for his own gain.

A thief will create a scenario to showcase his need for help or overcome an obstacle. Yet, his lack of the capacity to act forces those they steal from to become their savior. By forcing another soul into their darkness, the thief robs that psyche of its light as the victims can no longer focus on their own journey; they are robbed of their most precious opportunity of using time for their own path of wisdom. This distraction prevents one's evolution and forces both parties to remain in a state of imprisonment, disguised as an act of love, turning one thief into two.

When faced with the Gate of Choice, man must accept his choices and come to terms with the personality he has chosen to forge—even one of the thief. While some might claim that choosing deceit is wrong or needs to be changed, I would argue that in a world of balance, a choice is a direction. It is only when one is lost that the order of balance is disrupted, not when one has chosen his path. It is only then that man will find himself at eternity's gate, where he is faced with a closed door.

When man is shown his path and sees how far he diverged from his destiny, he will realize what lesson he failed to realize and when he fell victim to his EGO rather than establish the SELF. He will then realize why the gate hasn't opened and presented him an opportunity to pass.

Instead, he will have to travel the bridge back to a new vessel, forming new contracts (which we will discuss shortly) along the way. He makes this journey in hopes that it will help him overcome the new set of obstacles he will face as he now has a better view of the lessons he must experience, and, more importantly, overcome.

When man finds himself in front of a closed gate, he is robbed of the most powerful tool he had been given, his capacity for choice. He is no longer offered one.

PART III: The Choice

"Choice is man's greatest opportunity to overcome. It is the ultimate judgment man has to fulfill his greatest aspirations. It is only when man strips himself of such an opportunity that he no longer chooses to evolve. Instead, he falls victim to his shadows. While society imprisons the mind, time imprisons the vessel; it is choice that determines if we live a life as a Hero or a Thief." —Pejman Ghadimi

The choice man faces in each lifetime he experiences is the choice of living life as a Hero or as a Thief. We covered earlier the implications of each choice and its correlation with the evolution of our humanity. We will now break down the opportunities man has past the gate, once the choice has been made to overcome, and, more importantly what occurs when man overcomes all personalities and gives birth to the possibility of becoming the Superman.

The Universe: A Choice of Opportunities

Time and time again, man has aspired to seek out other planets, galaxies, and opportunities to answer if we are indeed alone in this universe and why we ended up here. So many questions arise as to who is the Divine Creator, what was His purpose in creating humanity, and if whether we are anything like His children. Are we the byproduct of a so-called God, a random event of happening, or is there a greater purpose to our existence in the cosmos?

Some argue that the earth is just one of the many ecosystems that exists into the universe, and others want to believe that we are so important that we are the only ones. Some of today's most powerful philosophers have also argued that God is dead, and it is in God's death that man has been conscious to take its place as a demi-god. Perhaps this reasoning is why man has a tendency to want to play God. It would make sense, since man is born in a control mechanism to assume that his greatest aspiration would evolve a certain level of control over his fellow man. All of these assumptions and theories hold valid to some point or another, but the real question we should be asking is, “Does it matter?”

In my quest for my own purpose, I have been met with countless opposition, including my own EGO persuading my SELF that, unless we can explain all aspects of our evolution and creation, the equation still remains unsolved. That quandary in itself could partially be why we will never solve such an equation in our current state of being.

It is possible, after all, that with each evolutionary step in new dimensions comes a new set of obstacles to learn and overcome, and that each realm holds its own gate to the next. One could perhaps spend an eternity trying to figure out how to get to the end of this journey. If we were to focus on the end of the journey rather than its experience, we would remain a prisoner to its limitations. One of the reasons philosophy and spirituality have suffered from separation from the majority of man has resulted from separation of the control mechanisms, creating no clear path for man to take.

Often the discussion of the power of a free mind, a free society, an evolved state of being, and even a greater cosmic purpose gives man very little transition and transcendence. Imagine a clear map of each state and its benefits in the United States, where no piece of the map connects the states to the others. A person embarking on a road trip may find themselves pleased or displeased of the state they find themselves in. Regardless, without connections between states, the traveler cannot progress to another state without a clear road or path to the next one.

I can understand why man for the most part seeks a path when searching for answers, rather than seeks to discover. The reason that so few people evolve through these various human phases stems from their inability to understand that the roads to such places do not preexist but are created through the evolution of the human himself.

So, once again, the questions we pose is, “Does it matter who the Creator is? Does it matter if He is dead? And, more importantly, does it matter if we do not know what the next realm holds?”

I ask this in not a rhetorical manner but from a place of self-reflection.

If man has yet to evolve to stage 2, then why worry about the road to stage 6? The same occurs in so many humans today when engaging in their state of creativity while questioning themselves on the basic ideas of:

Why create, if creation cannot be sold?

Why build a product if there is no path to wealth?

This mentality creates limitations in aspirations and connects aspiration (man’s greatest weapon of overcoming) to society (man’s greatest prison of overcoming). The result is a continuous battle that becomes counterproductive to evolution.

The more man focuses on having a perfect path to growth and evolution, the farther man steers away from his capacity to experience his own evolution. Reflecting on our previous talks as to how man grows and overcomes, you already understand how time has already taken its place, but it is the experience that deciphers your ability to stay on the evolutionary path of your Destiny Theory.

It is imperative that man finds in himself his ability to become the Hero of his own journey. He must realize that to be a Hero means to be present in one’s own experience today. He needs to focus on his ability to design his future, not read or predict it and to believe in his capacity to overcome whatever obstacles come his way.

In other words, focus on the experiences that will allow us to grow and to then grow from those experiences with the strength we acquired.

My very own journey was not based on a lucky break or even the combination of being at the right place at the right time. It was the byproduct of laying one brick at a time on the foundation of a home that I had yet to design. With each brick, I realized that the design looked closer to a home, empowering my aspiration to grow even more, while reminding myself that since I had made it that far, I would go even farther.

One could argue that if I had to first know everything about the home that never existed before I even laid a brick, I might never have built a house. We can also argue that I had to know what a home looked like to know the placement of my bricks. So much of life comes down to our capacity to experience our own evolution and to realize that what comes after the gate isn't as relevant as the journey to the gate. Living a life worth living is comprised of more experience and evolution than living a life for the sake of a reward associated with its completion.

If we understand that there is no end to man, but rather that man is a rope between Beast and Overman (as Nietzsche said), then we can conclude that the life we know isn't one that comes to completion with each cycle, but rather one that gives birth to a whole new experience filled with new opportunities.

We define the opportunities not by what rewards we can accumulate by its completion, but by the experiences we create, knowing we learned the core lesson of "choice" during our lifetime(s) here.

When man faces the Gate of Choice at the end of each cycle of his personality journey, he is given the opportunity to choose how he proceeds through the ecosystem. Those identified as thieves are sent back to attempt once more to master their choice patterns; however, those who have completed their journey—having forged a personality worth carrying on—are given an opportunity to forge new contracts before choosing to take control of a new vessel and reenter the ecosystem. Basically, they are designing their next Destiny Theory before experiencing it in the next vessel.

While man does not need to enter the ecosystem immediately with each cycle—as time in the fourth dimension is very different than time in our realm—he must eventually form new destiny circles. From there, he can reenter the realm in an effort to overcome all 48 personalities before moving forward and becoming a permanent resident of this new fourth-dimensional realm or perhaps choose his love for Earth, choosing instead to become the Superman.

Contracts: Forged Connections

We discussed earlier the opportunity of living as close to the Destiny Theory as possible and overcoming the distractions that prevent us from completing a full cycle and overcoming our personality. One of the misconceptions of occupying a vessel comes from the misunderstanding that our Destiny Theory is created *for* us, rather than *by* us. The reward for overcoming a personality is our opportunity to create our own Destiny Theory for the next personality to overcome. It's no different than picking your allies, enemies, and weapons for the next stage of a video game (the references to video games through this book as the third-dimensional realm on Earth represents a simulation for our psyche).

Remember that a forged personality that advances takes along its karmic energy. While that personality may not always remember its past circumstances, it does not have to relearn and readapt to all phases of life. Instead, the forged personality retains the traits from the prior forged personality it has built and carries it on to the next phase. The same applies to those who do not gain passage and must instead return, forced to carry with them the burden of the Thief instead.

Since time doesn't exist in its limiting state, man can see when making choices for his upcoming Destiny Theory what personality he wishes to overcome in his next phase. He creates the roadmap of his new experience, a map of his Destiny Theory, and identifies the obstacles he will most likely encounter. In addition to such obstacles, man will form contracts in this time with other individuals whom he believes will hold an opportunity to help on his journey.

Each of these contracts represents an opportunity to allow the interactions of certain individuals with another during each lifetime. This is why we meet people whom we seem to have known our entire life even though we just met them. They are predetermined interactions that must occur in order for shifts to occur in the completion of the personality. It could be a friend, business partner, accomplice, or a love interest. Whoever it is, that person holds a place in your timeline. If you have overcome the personality, you are creating such contracts from the SELF. On the other hand, the Thief believes to be creating such contracts. In reality, he does so through the EGO, creating more opportunities to be deceived than opportunities for wisdom, once more communicating through the EGO rather than SELF. This could translate to what you consider good luck or bad luck in meeting people.

The distinction between the contracts comes from the ability to decipher whether they stem from the SELF or the EGO. The SELF creates opportunities for evolution and transition, while the EGO prevents the experience of wisdom. In so doing, he robs the Thief who has accepted his EGO instead of overcoming it. We typically forge contracts with individuals who have held a role in our lives previously. For this reason, we keep finding one another time and time again. With each personality we experience, we encounter new opportunities and new personalities who then become part of our own ecosystem.

These relationships give way at times for thieves to experience the personalities of heroes. They recommit to the personal heroic journey that they once had abandoned. At times, heroes fall victim to thieves who sway them away from their journey and into the depth of distractions.

The basis of these contracts is to understand that we are all connected. Although we are not all equal in our capacity or how far we have come on our personal journey, these connections teach us that our relationships are not always based on our capacity for coexistence, but in co-understanding.

So, how do we form or rid ourselves of contracts we do not wish to keep in our lives?

I want to introduce you to a concept called the "Loop". Just like Destiny Theory, every contract is a circle of its own, having a start and conclusion. The difference is not one of the relationship and its outcome but rather a combination of the contents.

Imagine each loop contains energy. Two energies (two people) mix for a duration of time or through the completion of a task in time. If the loop is opened, the energies will mix and the experiences will occur. What matters just as much as opening loops to experience is closing the same loops to conclude them. Many times, man will open a loop, but never see its contents and energy fully mix before falling victim to a distraction, even if that distraction isn't always led by the hero of the story. How many have started businesses they have abandoned without failing? How many have met new individuals in whom they expressed interest in forging a contract but simply disappeared without the intent to let them know they no longer had interest? It sometimes is the byproduct of the other individual who, halfway through the journey, detached an open loop and carried on to another task.

This can be explained by business partners who never set out to finish what they started. Or they arrived at different outcomes that are not satisfactory to both; one person may have reached a desirable conclusion and the other continues to feel cheated. The less-than-satisfactory ending isn't one based on wisdom or deceit, but on unmet expectations. The result is more about the person's ability to close their internal loop than allowing a third-dimensional action to see its completion.

Many will leave such a loop open, not realizing that, by not completing a full cycle and ending what started, one will never graduate past that specific contract. One may experience the same energy in their life today and in the future under the context that a familiar feeling leads to a relationship to close an old contract. The same can be described about love by having a relationship where one cheated and experienced guilt as a result, while the other partner moved forward and had a great life. In this scenario, one partner's expectation was never met and experienced a feeling of void from being unable to overcome love without that contract that was once opened and not closed.

Without closure, the person struggles for progression. He may eventually find ways in future personalities to attempt to reconnect for the sake of closing such loops. This concept can lead to familiar faces, a feeling of comfort, a smile that makes you happier than others. The same can be said about broken contracts, creating a random feeling of distrust, betrayal, and even anger when, in reality, the person standing in front of you has done little to warrant such a reaction. The more broken or unfinished contracts exist in one life, the more distractions could arise in the next, causing a dangerous mix for the focus of one soul's opportunity for evolution.

The saying, "we don't always choose who we love but how we love", comes from the mechanics of meeting an old lover we haven't yet experienced in our latest personality.

Consider completed loops to be the fulfillment of a contract. If a loop is closed, the contract is closed and the connection is severed. If the connection is made and the loop not closed, something went wrong and created a rift that left unfinished business.

Even in cases where loops are closed, we can sense a level of familiarity. Those closed loops are now part of our forged personalities and carry on into the next realm, past the gate. This is partly why you might be in love with certain people and, while you may not have a romantic love interest, you can still feel a sincere sense of love. You need to hold that person near. Even though you may never have met them, they may have in a previous opportunity held the key to your safety, for example. So, a dependency exists that cannot be explained in the third-dimensional space.

For those who want to rid themselves of certain people or feelings, it becomes key to not overpromise or keep connections open that do not matter. Imagine a partner who constantly warrants your anger without resolve. Yet, you choose to keep that person in your life rather than severe that relationship in its entirety.

You are keeping the loops open. In the simplest form, you can relate this to the idea of open promises you do not intend to keep. You may meet a person who tells you that it would make sense to reconnect or spend time together. You hold no interest in doing that, yet you leave the idea open. Instead of the open promise, you could respond by denying the invitation. However, the majority of humanity fears the pain that comes with any level of rejection and, therefore, agrees to the request absolutely no intention of following through, rather than simply reject it, therefore not opening a loop. This inability to say “no” creates a magnitude of open loops that become the key to the distractions, in turn, prevent the evolution of man.

While you can form such contracts prior to entering the next circle of destiny, it will be up to you to ensure the formed contracts end up as closed loops during your tenure in the third dimension. They must be closed for each personality you attempt to overcome. By ensuring and paying attention to closing these loops, so you do not forever stay connected in a prison of time.

Final Choice: The Choice to Love

The idea of theological evolution is to overcome one's SELF and evolve. With each personality, man comes closer to overcoming himself and shedding his vessel to occupy time, not space, as a fourth-dimensional being. Each personality mastered presents an opportunity to move one step closer to the overcoming of man and the ability to once and for all shed our vessel and no longer be bound by Earth-based laws that define our existence. When man gives shape to his being, he no longer needs the illusion of shape (EGO) to be recognized by others.

When a Destiny Circle is completed and man has overcome his personality, he is given an opportunity to return to a new vessel, carrying his karmic personality onwards. If man chooses, he may spend time as a fourth-dimensional being in an attempt to learn, prior to returning to another personality. Do not forget that, while time here on Earth is defined by the concept of a 12-hour cycle, time in the fourth dimension is defined by personality. This means, if we transpose the zodiac calendar over a 12 -hour cycle, it would translate to each personality being no more than 15 minutes (one quadrant) of their time. This would mean that each 100-year cycle of ours is basically 15 minutes of theirs. While this may seem hard to believe, it is the same as a butterfly that may only live 17 days but, in its own perception, feels like 100 years, since they complete a whole lifecycle in 17 days that takes us 100 years to do.

The question now remains, what happens when someone completes and overcomes the 48 personalities and forges their final personality for the Gate of Choice?

Once they have overcome their time on earth in its entirety, man has two choices.

He can remain as masters of time in the fourth dimension and carry onwards or to stay in the third and help others transition to the fourth dimension.

While humanity is filled with darkness, it is also filled with love. For every act of hatred comes an opportunity to love. *For every act of deceit, comes an opportunity to love wisdom.*

The idea of love in society is driven by the commitment and connection that man experiences. To the Higher Man, love is language, an opportunity to give worth to what has no value.

In the end, love is the highest form of alchemy, to create and to give value not to one's self but to others.

We broke down earlier that man should never attempt to help others without having helped himself first (not to be confused with man should not perform acts of kindness through his life). Man needs to reach a higher level of consciousness that enables him to understand how to love himself first so that he may truly love others. He should not build a dependency on others that is driven by the EGO. These relationships can harm others, causing all to create more EGO.

Love is the universal language that transcends all dimensions. From the love one shares for another person to a passion one shares to unite people around their creation, love is the silent driver and connector of all energies. This is partially the reason that the heart chakra is the hardest one to unlock and keep under control; more importantly, the heart chakra should be the most precious and final one so that it can regulate all internal and external energy the vessel produces.

When one falls in love with Earth, one is given the opportunity to carry on yet another mission here in the ecosystem instead of outside of it, past those personalities that are not focused on overcoming themselves. This mission is to help fellow man evolve into the next realm. This task is particularly important as the balance of all life on and off the Earth requires a commitment to wisdom in order to offset the amount of deceit that has chosen to no longer evolve.

These individuals, known as “thieves” and “slaves”, find themselves attached to their distractions and comfort. They have abandoned the idea of their purpose, which is to evolve.

As a result, Earth is overpopulated by individuals who no longer wish to grow but rather prevent others from becoming free, as they themselves are forever enslaved to masters they cannot overcome. This is why we have so many who belong to the Herd—individuals who want equality and prevent personality from following its evolutionary cycle.

To make the ultimate sacrifice and choose to love your fellow men more than your own evolution—past the forging of your personality—means to delay the opportunity for evolution as a master of time. So, you remain on Earth as a guardian of it, also known as becoming the Superman.

PART IV: The Superman

"I teach you the superman. Man is something that should be overcome. What have you done to overcome him? All gods are dead, now we want the superman to live." (Thus Spoke Zarathustra)

The Beginning of The End: The Birth of The Superman

Zarathustra once said that humanity would eventually find itself consumed by distractions, enslaved my masters, and focused more on entertainment than enlightenment.

He said that a time like that would come when the fate of all would be in the hands of the unqualified few, when man would be more interested in deceit than wisdom, and when slavery would become a mental barrier rather than a physical one.

Atlantis, Persia, and Rome all suffered the same fate at a time when most of its population chose deceit and comfort over wisdom and evolution. This created an imbalance that collapsed entire civilizations.

Will we face the same fate?

In the Gate of Choice, we have identified many definitions that can help us live a more meaningful life geared towards theological evolution, rather than one bound to worship. Many will seek to use these definitions as a roadmap to what to do or not do in order to find societal success, rather than to understand how to overcome. While many of these definitions will enable the ability to grow in a societal setting, these definitions are not there to help you find monetary success.

Instead, they are there to enable you to understand a new perspective on truth, one where we understand that during our lifetime here on Earth, we must once more find a path to the Superman. At the very least, we will have endured the hardship of becoming the bridge for the Superman for those who follow in our existence.

Regardless that you believe we are in a simulation, part of an evolutionary cycle, or in the middle of a cosmic battle, each of us must realize the power and importance of our capacity for growing our wisdom. We can and should not be prisoners of internal and external boundaries, regardless of whether they are self-created or not.

The Superman is man's ultimate personality, the possibility of what man can be and of the integration of a forged personality with a vessel that can support its power and depth. A man not defined by fears and boundary, not bound to masters, but committed to mastery. Not swayed by deceit but whose wisdom extends beyond his physical years. A being who no longer sees time as a prison but as an opportunity.

In this final section, we will uncover what the Superman is and why his existence is an important step in man's evolutionary path.

The Superman: A Guardian of Time

In the beginning of *The Gate of Choice*, we reviewed the string theory, the ability to understand that dimensions can ultimately be linked to shapes. In using such logic, we can categorize consciousness and how its existence in thoughts is linked to its existence in the third dimension. We determined that an insect is a one-dimensional being, existing as **one point** at a time. The animal is a two-dimensional one, only computing **one motion** at a time from one place to another, also drawn as a **line**. The two-dimensional being simply cannot move freely in space as it lacks the notion of time, so it is limited to one motion at a time. In other words, a lion cannot go from point A to B to C in a premeditated manner. Its motion is always limited to

Point A to B, when B becomes A once more with each range of motion. The limitation of the animal is based in function, not comprehension, therefore limiting its understanding to the third dimension of motion in a space only.

The human, on the other hand, operates in a third-dimensional **space** but is bound to the fourth dimension, also referred to as a **circle.** During one lifecycle, a clear path to evolution exists. From a confined space, like a square, to an expandable space, like a circle, we see a clear evolution in the very same life cycle, partly because man is both vessel and psyche. We cannot clearly see a definition from a lion to a human but can see man evolve from a prisoner to a master. This transition occurs because we no longer seek a visual to associate with the idea of transformation, rather only the *experience* of the thoughts associated with it. **By evolving, man does not have a stronger** more muscular **design; instead man evolves in his mental and energy state** once more proving that evolution isn't always a physical transformation.

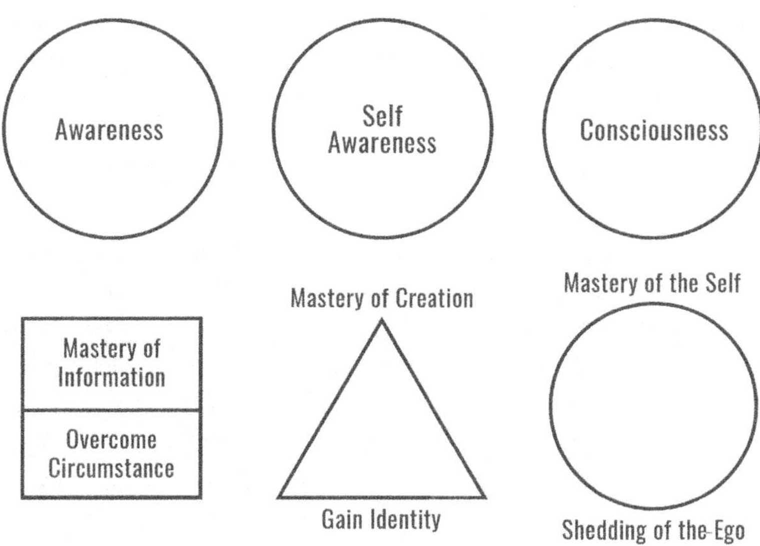

Before we carry on, I want to point out that shapes and geometry matter in the idea of evolution. The purpose of this book is to help you define your own path to the Superman. In order to understand such evolution, let's review what we learned so far between *Third Circle Theory*, *RADIUS,* and *The Gate of Choice*.

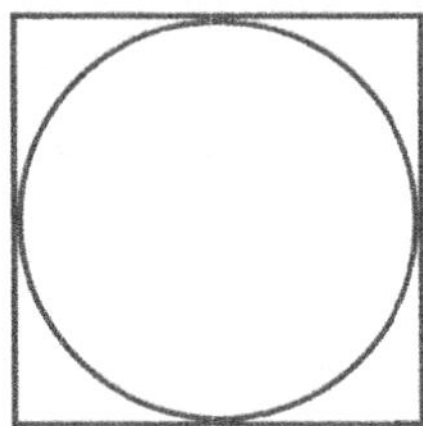

Imagine a square with a circle in it. It is limiting with hard edges. It presents a beginning and an ending, and it can expand but will always carry its shape of beginning and ending. The square represents the boundary of an imprisoned mind (represented by the circle inside the square), one that is bound by the rules and belief of society. This square can be identified as the vessel and man's belief that he is one with his body.

Now, imagine a circle by itself and its meaning, it can be looked at as expandable, never limited to a beginning or ending. It is infinite and continuing. The circle, which represents the psyche, is a prisoner of the vessel. A circle trapped in a square means that it can only expand at the pace of the square, never overcoming it. The triangle (which represents creativity, mastery, and entrepreneurship) is needed to transition from the imprisoned SELF to the one leading the expansion of the soul. This conductor of energy enables the SELF to break free of the boundary of the square.

In other words, man is no longer a prisoner of his vessel but a master of it.

The triangle in the photo below represents the transfer of energy that allows man to transition from an imprisoned mind (the square) to an expandable one (the circle). The creation, mastery, and alchemy play the transitional role, where the Gate of Choice graphic comes from, a reengineered version of the alchemy symbol adapted to a more modern world.

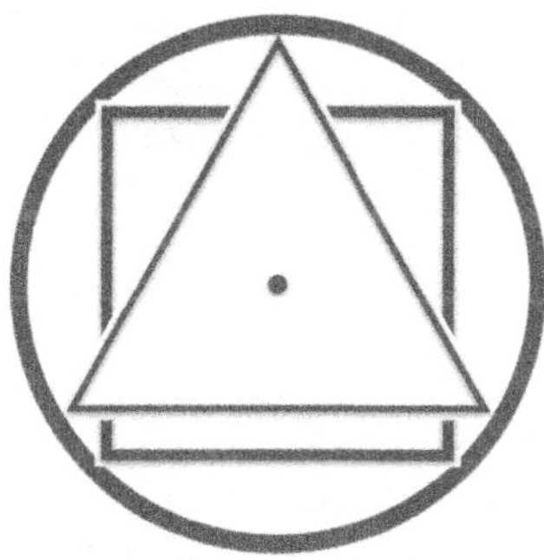

The triangle is very important. In *Radius*, the triangle represents one's ability to connect their skill, love, and confidence and to grow them into their talent, passion, and belief, giving birth to Creation, which we discussed, is the driver of evolution. Unity around Creation gives birth to mastery; mastery enables reputation; and reputation allows man to understand that he is no longer a prisoner of time

(the fourth dimension). Time is man's ultimate prison, because it is the guarantor that man will not remain trapped in a defective vessel for his entire existence. Yet even when man has discovered how to effectively manage and control his vessel, his physical existence is still in question. It will eventually end. So, how can man beat time? Man cannot, but the Superman can. The difference between the Superman and ma, is the Superman's evolutionary state of turning one's Destiny Circle into a sphere.

A **sphere** encompasses time, space, and continuity. The sphere allows the psyche to operate in time and space, rather than in a space bound by time. The Superman can inhabit any vessel without forgetting who he is and the personality associated with it, giving him the continuity of life and the power of choice at his command, rather than after his evolutionary cycle. If we can understand the time and space continuum—how we are experiencing time at a slower pace than its occurrence—then we are already in a Higher Being's ecosystem. Their existence is occurring at the same time as our own, the same as our existence's impact on the snail that exists in our ecosystem and yet has no correlation to our lives.

If we can conclude that our evolution is not a two-fold approach but rather a three-fold one, we can then conclude that our existence here on Earth is only relative to time because the Supermen are and have always been here with us. Their presence is the dominant controller of time, timelines, and energy in our space. They enable us to experience time at a significantly slower speed than its occurrence and so comes the ultimate question:

Who and where is the Superman?

When man has chosen to become the Superman past his evolutionary capacity, then he has chosen to love mankind and help its evolution. While becoming the Superman may have a supernatural definition to it, it isn't so much a position of strength as a position of protection or guardianship.

The Superman's role is to guard the evolutionary cycle of life and to ensure that mankind lives on, so that those who are in his ecosystem can complete their very own Destiny Circles. The role of the Superman has always been to protect his fellow man against their own extinction.

Time and time again through history, the Superman has existed amongst us, silently protecting the direction of the future by intervening in our day-today lives without us even knowing it. The lack of awareness often leads us to blame karma or luck on bizarre situations that occur yet force us to remain on the path of discovery, creativity, or overcoming. The Superman has always been listening to those who can manifest their thoughts in the ecosystem. He has helped carry the link between those who control time and those who impact it, living as a new god here on Earth— not one who asks for worship, but rather one who helps others evolve.

Final Words

A Story: An Opportunity for a Hero to Arise

As discussed throughout this entire book, definitions matter. Generalizations are definitions lost in time, rather than guidelines meant to help us evolve. Most of humanity gains its value and belief system at an age of pre-consciousness from parents, friends, guardians, or influences. As a result, they are born into a state of imprisonment, such as religion or government. They have never been given the chance to choose, imprisoned by a boundary of control mechanisms geared to prevent a state of evolution that prevents a free mind.

In essence, as a child, man doesn't have the power of choice. The direction is chosen for him. As man evolves to a state of consciousness, he is given the opportunity to choose between seeking wisdom (learning about his religion, government, or other control mechanisms as a means of structure) or choose deceit (the acceptance of an illusion of comfort and security) by continuing to follow the guidelines of the prison created for him.

The definitions in this book are definitions of abstract words driven by the absence of a control mechanism. My intent is for you to understand their universal meanings. The broader the opportunity for interpretation, the more opportunity exists for man to find his own answers, and the farther he pushes away from the idea of established values and worship, and more towards the idea of seeking wisdom.

Wisdom is man's ultimate weapon to re-spark his aspiration. Wisdom can give birth to one's commitment to creation and mastery, two components that are unfortunately becoming a rarity these days as the need to belong and the need for acceptance overshadow man's capacity for individuality and personality.

Time is the one boundary that man can never break free of, as it is the guiding principle that enables a third-dimensional being to give meaning to their life by forging a personality and leaving a reputation behind. What man can overcome is mastery of the control of time till he has the ability to transcend its control by no longer existing in the space that is controlled by it.

The transition from a state of third- to fourth-dimensional awareness isn't one of physical mutation or evolution, but rather one of choice. It is one's ability to manage not just the internal shadows and light, not just wisdom and belief, but also revelation and application.

For the longest time, man has been warned of the upcoming collapse of the western world. From the decline in heroism to man giving up on his highest aspirations, we have been warned by countless philosophers and historians of the dangers of continuing on such a path of decline and renouncing our need to evolve. We can blame this for the most part on the masters who have disguised our external evolution as an internal one.

In short, they created a falsified sense of evolution to satisfy our EGOS, rather than give birth to our consciousness. In other words, they have expanded man's imprisoned mind from a small cell to a slightly larger one. From giving people a falsified sense of importance through capitalism, to the idea that man was carrying on God's mission through his obedience, civilization is now at a tipping point where each and every one of us must make a choice: to give in to revelation or to fall victim to application.

Application is man's opportunity to follow instructions. Think of application as deploying what you have learned to provide structure and guidance to grow. While application is a powerful concept in evolution, it is powerful due to its push for man to use another man's structure to gain his very own path of revelation. Application without revelation leads to worship. You could say that many of the most successful businessmen today suffer from a lack of spirituality because of their application versus their choice of revelation.

Revelation is man's opportunity to not be told what to do but rather shape his own belief and value system, one that enables him the aspiration to overcome each of his personalities and rid himself of his vessel, forging a final personality onward. The opportunity to use the collective level of information and awareness to overcome himself, to give birth to his true cosmic consciousness. Revelation without application, however, leads to a state of imprisonment. Many of the reasons that philosophers suffer from a disconnect to society is their choice of revelation over their choice of application.

Man's evolution comes down to choosing the experience of life and the opportunity to overcome one's personality, rather than seek comfort in a selfish attempt to simply stay here on Earth. Making such a choice comes from the ability to combine the idea of revelation with application instead choose between the two paths. The path of revelation accepts that the Destiny Theory and the path one has assigned himself prior to entering his vessel is one's personal choice of the experiences they have set for themselves in order to complete and overcome their personality.

It is also to accept that we enter our vessels with each and every opportunity, carrying forward the karmic rewards or debt owed from our previous personalities. The path of application is our ability to set self-created parameters, known as values and beliefs, to overcome our revelation and complete our personality. Without application, one loses grounding; without revelation, one loses aspiration. It is why one of man's greatest opportunities to ensure his completion of his Destiny Theory is to be self-conscious and capable of impacting his revelation and application on a continuous level. Man must not only be able to overcome himself and the obstacles his personality faces but he must learn to use application to force change as necessary to ensure he is capable of living through the experience of wisdom rather than worship.

Think of one who struggles through the imprisonment of his deceit by giving in to the inability to control his need for alcohol. While he may meet a partner in life who pushes him to abandon his habits, he is living the path of application. However, when man consciously identifies his own deceit and chooses to overcome his revelation through forcing his own application, he overcomes his need to give in to deceit. The idea of drinking in itself isn't an issue here, but rather man's inability to overcome his own need, therefore creating a false sense of overcoming through alcohol. We can argue here that having a partner help you move past deceit sounds better than the falsified notion of overcoming through a substance. Both are the same. They are, in the end, a catalyst induced by the environment to create change. The true change that will impact man's personality must come from his choice, not from his environment.

Man, in this day, struggles from the inability to commit to the idea of his very own evolution. He is significantly more concerned about his comfort than he is of his overcoming. This is partly the result of thousands of years of mental imprisonment, known as religion, government, and capitalism. In each of these evolutionary phases of society and life, man has once more fallen victim to giving in to a boundary of control, rather than overcoming them and reaching for his highest aspirations. Man has gotten by, being a Hero in his environment rather than the Hero of his own journey. While society has become a vital control mechanism to the function of man here on Earth, it has also become man's greatest challenge to overcome in his third-dimensional form, in essence becoming man's path of application.

One's capacity to control his energy source and one's ability to connect to a path of revelation in the fourth dimension is only as useful as being able to connect such revelation to the applications of the third dimension. More simply, when you consider yourself spiritual without the ability to leverage such spirituality to take action here, in the present experience, you experience a dangerous form of escapism.

This has become the greatest threat to man leveraging an opportunity to evolve into a higher state of consciousness and instead expect others to lead the way. Thus, you create a state of worship disguised as a path to evolution. In this book, I hope that you have found no application and no revelation, but rather an opportunity to overcome the definitions that have forever bound man to worship, rather than evolve. Choosing the path of application without revelation leads to a life lived through the EGO; choosing a path of revelation without application means to live a life of worship.

It is with those words that I leave you with an opportunity to overcome yourself. I also leave with one of the most important lines from the only philosopher who connected philosophy to psychology, reminding us that aspiration is only as important as the choices we make to overcome our greatest fear and push to become the final hero in our own stories.

"The time has come when man will no more shoot the arrow of his longing out over mankind, and the string of his bow will have forgotten how to twang. When the hunger for heroism dies in the culture, the cultures begin to die, too—but by my love and hope, I entreat you: Do not reject the hero in your soul! Keep holy your highest hope!" —Frederick Nietzsche (Thus spoke Zarathustra)

Words of Gratitude

As I sit here and watch the future of man, I can only watch in hopes that more men will understand their roles here on Earth and choose to take on life rather than be taken by it, giving birth to their very own bridges. I wish that more men will answer the call and rise to a new state of belief, understanding and seeking to redeem their reputation over their EGO. I hope that more men will work to forge their personalities, live out their Destiny Theory, and no longer hide behind the control of masters who have convinced us that obedience or worship is the ultimate salvation, and comfort the ultimate goal.

After all, the Higher Human exists within each of us, but it is our choice to ignore him for the luring call of the Herd, or to honor the Hero we can be by transcending ourselves and becoming bridges to the Superman, a new generation of men who no longer fear themselves, who no longer find contempt in the outside world, and who embody the character of those we once referred to as “gods”. More importantly, a new breed of man who will reestablish the balance of order in the universe, for our civilization is at risk of losing its capacity to govern itself; for that reason. they could become slaves to another civilization or simply face inevitable extinction. While time will take its course, we must ensure that our civilization will not outrun its time and be forgotten.

It is with immense pleasure that I leave you what I consider to be my masterpiece for you to experience and to overcome its definitions. I would be lying if I didn’t mention the incredible talent that inspired these words and pages.

I want to thank all the people in my life who took the time to remind me that my work mattered to them, and who enabled *Third Circle Theory* and

RADIUS to become part of their daily lives. It is because of people like you that I have the strength to continue helping people, despite the lurking shadows that doom most.

I want to thank my mother, Shahla Monsefan, who forever has and always will be my guardian and my connection to Earth. It is in our past life that we formed a contract and in this one that you have honored it, not only protecting me during my youth, but also positioning me to understand the power of choice in life and its impact on my reputation. *Third Circle Theory*, *RADIUS* and *The Gate of Choice* are as much what I leave behind as they are an imprint of your character.

I want to thank Rachael Alfonso for your courage and willingness to face the gate at a time where most would have run away and to have honored your contract in this lifetime as the transformer. I am thankful for your support during this very difficult process. I am excited to continue to watch your growth over the years to come and hope that you do not fall victim to your shadows as you undertake the beginning of your very own journey.

I want to thank Calvin Knight, a man who entered my life as a student, turned friend, and became a facilitator for the Higher Man to find this work. While the average man fights his shadow in hopes of finding light, may he find your light as a guide to finding his true SELF. I wish I could say our journey is coming to an end, but it is now the beginning of our contract and I am excited to have you along for the journey. A difficult road awaits us, but one I am sure we will travel together.

I want to thank Alan Dang who, for the last decade, has not only supported my visions and decisions no matter how crazy they were, but also matured into a Higher Human, an incredible businessman and, most importantly, a father. It is perhaps with this new generation that we can change the direction for humanity. I wish I could tell you that our work is now done and you can just live life, but reality is that our friendship, brotherhood, and impact are only starting to see the light of day.

I want to thank Andrew Goodman, someone who gave me the support I needed to be able to focus on the core of my work, rather than the marketing of it. It has been a pleasure watching you grow into the person you are today. It is with confidence that we enter this next phase of our life, no longer as friends but as brothers.

I want to acknowledge Navid Norouzi for who you are, giving me the opportunity in this lifetime to close out our contract and more importantly give you the opportunity to overcome your own personality. Many of our earlier life conversations allowed me to overcome my fear of accepting my cosmic purpose and push for my greatest aspirations.

I want to thank Mary, a guide whose intervention facilitated the opportunity for me to overcome my own EGO and enabled me to face my own gate. It was in our conversations that I was reminded and given an opportunity to learn to view my own Destiny Theory.

Finally, I want to recognize the people whom society has forgotten in favor of vanity. I want to recognize philosophers, stoics, and alchemists who had to live in their shadows in order to help others find their light.

This work is dedicated to all people who gave your physical lives for your reputation and who didn't give up on your beliefs of others while others gave up on you.

Made in the USA
Coppell, TX
05 October 2023